# INEXPENSIVE EXPERIENCE:
# CHAMPIONS TELL ALL

## MASTERS OF THE MENTAL GAME SERIES BOOK

*This book is being given to*

_____

*because I care about you and your success*

_____

## BRIAN M. CAIN, MS, CMAA

Brian Cain Peak Performance, LLC

## What Champions Are Saying About Brian Cain
### & *Inexpensive Experience, Champions Tell All*

*"The stories in the book allow you to step inside of their heads and see how they think. It is amazing that whether you are a mixed martial arts fighter or a softball player, the process for success is the same."*

**Lonni Alameda**
**Head Softball Coach,**
**Florida State University**

*"Hearing how various athletes apply the mental game principles that Cain teaches gives the reader a better understanding of the power that mental conditioning gives you as an athlete and as a person."*

**Rob Childress**
**Head Baseball Coach**
**Texas A&M University**

*"This book contains everything you need to know to become a Master of the Mental Game. Cain is an industry leader in Mental Conditioning and the stories of success he features here will greatly help you understand and appreciate how he has helped to advance the field."*

**Dr. Angus Mumford**
**Director of Mental Conditioning**
**IMG Academies, Bradenton, Florida, USA**

*"In order to get the most out of your potential, you must train physically and mentally with the best coaches in the world. Brian Cain is that coach when it comes to mental conditioning."*

**Rich "Ace" Franklin**
**Ultimate Fighting Championship**
**Former Middleweight World Champion**

*"If you are looking for an easy to read and easy to implement program for training your mental toughness, this book is exactly what you are looking for."*

**George Horton**
**Head Baseball Coach**
**The University of Oregon**
**2004 NCAA National Champion**

*"Cain has done it again. Another absolute for a coach's and athlete's library. This book takes you inside the minds of champions in sport and in life."*

**Patrick Murphy**
**Head Softball Coach**
**The University of Alabama**
**2012 NCAA National Champion**

*"If you are looking to take your performance to the next level, Cain will help you get there."*

**Firas Zahabi**
**Mixed Marital Arts Trainer**
**Tristar Gym, Montreal, Canada**

*"Cain's books are easy for to read and effective for coaches and athletes to use. We have them all."*

**Kevin Ozee**
**Athletic Director, Southlake Carroll ISD, TX**
**2013 National HS AD of the Year**

# Inexpensive Experience:
# Champions Tell All

## MASTERS OF THE MENTAL GAME SERIES BOOK

## BRIAN M. CAIN, MS, CMAA

Brian Cain Peak Performance, LLC

Brian M. Cain, MS, CMAA
Peak Performance Coach
Peak Performance Publishing
Brian Cain Peak Performance, LLC

*Inexpensive Experience:*
*Champions Tell All*

A Masters of the Mental Game Series Book
©2013 by Brian M. Cain. MS, CMAA

Printed in the United States of America
Edited by: Justin Dedman
Cover design & book layout: Nu-Image Design
Illustrations: Nicole Ludwig and Greg Pajala
Photography: Don Whipple and Paul Lamontangue

Brian M. Cain, MS, CMAA

*Inexpensive Experience:*
*Champions Tell All*

A Masters of the Mental Game Series Book
Brian M. Cain, MS, CMAA
Library of Congress Control Number: 2013942371
ISBN: 978-0-9830379-9-6

# PREFACE

There are two types of experience in the world: expensive and inexpensive. Expensive experience is trying to learn everything you need to know to be successful on your own, a process that is destined to keep you from reaching your true potential. Inexpensive experience, on the other hand, is learning from other's experiences which sharpens your learning curve and helps you to achieve your true potential as quickly as possible.

*Inexpensive Experience: Champions Tell All* is the inexpensive experience from World Champions, Olympic medalists, Players of The Year and MVPs that you need to speed up your mental toughness learning curve and start sharing a similar success.

These great athletes share their success stories in using Brian Cain's mental conditioning system. This book is the fourth book in the *Masters of the Mental Game Series*. When read and put into action, the secrets of success shared on these pages will change your career and change your life.

This is not a sports book. This is a book on excellence and success. The aim of this book is to provide you with insight into the minds of the world's greatest athletes and let you know how they think so that if you train yourself to think the same way, you can have a similar success and reach your true potential.

This is a book for people looking for simple yet effective ways to reach peak performance. This book will not go into theory or research, but is itself a body of research in which you are able to learn from the inexpensive experience of others on what works in the field of mental conditioning and peak performance.

Here is to your domination of every day and learning how to play your best when it means the most.

# DEDICATION

This book is dedicated to the eleven amazing people who shared their experiences with me so I could share them with you.

Rich, you are an inspiration to us all for pursuing your dreams and having the faith to give up a truly amazing career as a teacher for what you dreamed of doing as a competitor.

Matt, you are living proof that success is a choice and making the decision to be excellent is a lifestyle, not an event.

Casey, you are an Olympic hero and someone who embraces the adversity that baseball gives you with a relentless, positive energy and a drive to do what is right at all times. Stay on your path, the hurdles put in front of you are not to keep you from your goals, but to see how badly you really want them.

Ben, you are the definition of will over skill and hard work paying off. You set the standard for work ethic and fundamental execution for all of college baseball to follow.

Justin, you have played every position on the field in one game, a feat that may never be accomplished again. More impressive is your resilience and ability to stay focused on your goals.

Josh, your senior season gives hope to all of the players out there who have greatness inside of them but just have not shown it YET! Your career continues to give us all hope, Hold On Possibilities Exist.

Bryan, your fight to live is an inspiration to me every day. You are a fighter, a one pitch warrior who will not be defeated on or off the field and have overcome more adversity in your life

2                          www.briancain.com

already than most face in their entirety. Keep telling your story, it is one that moves people to fight and shows the true power of the mental game and what coaches are really for, to teach life lessons through sport.

Ryan, you have been there since day one as a teammate and best friend of mine on the little league fields of Williamstown, Massachusetts. Keep giving back to the game. Your passion for teaching is contagious and life changing.

Amanda, your resilience and desire to improve yourself showed the power that lives inside people. You never quit, you just kept battling and showed how changing your perspective will change your reality. Keep teaching that critical life lesson in your classroom and on the field.

Mike, your commitment to excellence and understanding of all aspects of the game has made you a great player and will make you a fantastic coach. Keep pursuing the dream and keep empowering others to do the same.

Thank you all for sharing your stories and experiences. You are positively affecting lives of people whom you will never meet. That will help your legacy live on forever.

# ACKNOWLEDGMENTS

It is with sincere and deep appreciation that I acknowledge the support and guidance of the following people who helped make this book possible.

Special thanks to Tom Murphy, Firas Zahabi, Jorge Gurgel, Jim Schlossnagle, Tim Corbin, Steve Smith, Jack Dahm, Lee Toole, Kyla Holas, Kevin Sneddon, Dave Serrano, Todd Whitting, Vito and Debbie Cameron, Ken Ravizza and Deb Deakins.

I would also like to acknowledge you and your commitment to excellence in reading and applying the teachings in this book.

By signing your name below you are dedicating yourself to this book and to applying the inexpensive experience you will learn by reading this book.

I,_____ (print your name), have been given everything I need to become excellent. I am fully capable of living the life of my dreams and leaving this world a better, more excellent place. I will apply the lessons I learn though the inexpensive experience of the eleven individuals in this book.

I am devoting myself to the pursuit of excellence, and I realize that this journey has no finish line. I am committing to the creation of a positive legacy. I realize that the legacy I leave will be defined by what I do today, because it is the sum of my todays that constitutes my career and my life.

I realize that my legacy will be further defined by the relationships I develop and how I treat my teammates in life. Thus, I am hereby committed to improving the relationships in my life and my greater community by improving myself.

Every day, I will wake up and make the inspired commitment to improve myself and to take steps closer to my dreams in an attempt to become the person I desire to be.

I realize that each day I will not be as excellent as I want to be and not as excellent as I am going to be, but I will work every day to make progress and to be more excellent than I was the day before.

I hereby sign my name below to certify my commitment to the pursuit of excellence!

_____

**YOUR NAME**                          **DATE**

**www.BrianCain.com/experience For BONUS Mental Conditioning Material & FREE Peak Performance Training Tools To Help You Become A Master of The Mental Game.**

# CONTENTS

## 5. JUSTIN TOOLE

## 8. RYAN CAMERON
### No Place In Baseball For The Passive Pitcher ...........**139**

## 9. AMANDA CRABTREE
### Softball Pitcher Uses Mental Game To Turn Career Around & Leads Country In Strikeouts Per Game.....171

# AUTHOR'S NOTE

The intent of the author in writing this book in the Masters of the Mental Game Series was to share the stories of some of the best competitors I have worked with. I wanted you to hear their story in their words and learn what some of the best are thinking on a daily basis.

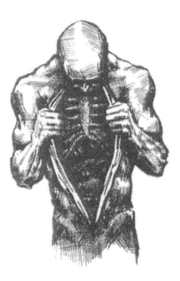

If you can develop a similar champion's mindset like they have, that will help you to work like they work and that will lead you to have success like they have had. Enjoy the stories as they share with you what has worked, what has not and what you can do to be at your best when it means the most.

The photo to the left illustrates taking a look inside of yourself to search for life's answers. Please enjoy the journey into self of the 11 champions featured in this book.

***www.BrianCain.com/experience***
***For BONUS Mental Conditioning Material &***
***FREE Peak Performance Training Tools To Help***
***You Become A Master of The Mental Game.***

# CHAPTER #1

*T*his interview is between Brian Cain and Former Ultimate Fighting Championship Middleweight World Champion Rich Franklin. Franklin discusses how the mental aspects of mixed martial arts are often overlooked and taken for granted, and are one of the most important aspects of fight preparation.

## TRAINING IS PHYSICAL, FIGHTING IS MENTAL

Preparation is 90% physical and 10% mental, yet when the fight comes, it is 90% mental and 10% physical. I have had a very successful career and feel that a large part of that has been due to my physical preparation, but also my mental preparation.

When you wake up on Friday with the fight on Saturday and you go to weigh-ins , the next 24 to 48 hours is a huge mental game.

Many athletes think their mental preparation is working harder physically and they don't know about mental imagery, breathing exercises, recognizing signal lights, or that confidence is a choice and the importance of acting different than how you feel. I don't think many athletes, even at the highest level, have a mental game plan for peak performance.

## CONFIDENCE FROM PHYSICAL WORK IS KEY

I know that if I work myself harder than I think is possible, then I will have the confidence going into the fight knowing that there's nothing more I can do to get ready physically. Going into a fight you have to have confidence that you have done all of the work physically to prepare or all of the mental work will not help you. I think you have to do the physical first and then the mental, but if you are going to be consistent over time, you must do both.

**CAIN'S COACHING POINT:**
**Are you taking confidence from your physical work? What can you do better in training this week to increase your confidence in preparation?**

_____

_____

## TRAINING THE RELAXATION RESPONSE

Doing the mental imagery and the breathing exercises outside of the gym helps you to train the relaxation response that takes over when you walk to the cage on fight night. When you can control your relaxation response, you get that relaxed intensity feeling and that relaxed confidence that "I've been here before." You have the feeling that you have already gone through this before and deserve to go out there and be successful. It helps you to deal with the anxiety that you always feel on fight night.

**www.BrianCain.com/experience For BONUS Mental Conditioning Material & to link to Cain's podcast so you can download your relaxation training audios.**

## ALWAYS ANXIETY AND SELF-DOUBT

No matter what you do, there will always be some anxiety and self-doubt on fight night. No matter how confident you are, there is always going to be a fear that you can lose the fight. The mental imagery helps you to deal with that anxiety the night of the fight. By the time I walk into cage, I feel like I have been there before. The mental imagery does help with the anxiety, but it will always be there. You have to learn to embrace it.

Sometimes that anxiety can take control of you. What the mental game does is give you something to go to. You can act different than how you feel or as you may have heard, "fake it till you make it.

## THE BUTTERFLIES NEVER GO AWAY

I thought that working with a mental conditioning coach would help all the anxiety and all the fear and to go away, and I wouldn't have to deal with it anymore. I liked the thought of that. I liked the thought of not being afraid before a fight. Nobody wants to feel that anxiety. Nobody wants to feel butterflies in the stomach and all the emotions that come before a fight. What I have learned is that those feelings, the butterflies and the anxiety are never going to go away. Those feelings are just a part of the competition. I have learned that there is a difference between letting those feelings control you to the point where it affects your performance negatively and channeling those feelings and energy to help take your performance to another level.

You want to get the butterflies to fly in formation. The anxiety is always going to be there, but start to view that anxiety and view those butterflies as a positive, not a negative. Physiologically, you have the butterflies because the blood is being pulled out of your stomach, and going into your extremities, helping you to get ready for battle.

Embrace that feeling you get before a fight. There are not many times in your life where you get those butterflies and get that feeling. Those feelings mean you are ready to go and it's time to reap the benefits from all of your preparations and all of the hard work.

No matter what happens, I'm going to be nervous in my fight. I just had to learn to like those feelings. They are not going to go away physiologically. It's reassuring knowing that the body has a physiological response to stress and there is not much I can do about it but embrace it and run towards it versus away from it. I'm nervous when I'm sitting in the locker room and I know that I'm nervous and I know that I'm scared, but to know that I am not the only one who feels this way and that there is not something wrong with me has made a big difference.

## CONTROL WHAT YOU CAN CONTROL

One of the foundations of the mental game is being able to control what you can control, staying inside your circle of control and taking all those things outside of your circle of control and letting them go. I think one thing that athletes experience, whether it's fighters, baseball, football, basketball players or golfers, is that when they look back at poor performance it is often the result of getting caught on things they couldn't control?

Before working with Brian Cain, most of my stress, anxiety and concerns going into a fight were outside of my control. I would get stuck on what people were going to think if I lost or did not finish the fight. I have learned that what other people say and what other people think are outside of my control and I can't worry about things outside of my control.

## OTHER FIGHTERS SHOULD TRY MENTAL CONDITIONING

I think any fighters who are out there that want to take their performance to the next level should try out mental conditioning and sport psychology. It's going to give them an edge and they should start tapping into that edge right now.

## SURROUND YOURSELF WITH GREAT COACHES

Knowing what I know now and having been around MMA for a long time, I feel like I am knowledgeable in a lot of aspects of fight preparation. I know a lot about fighting; I know a lot about boxing and wrestling, nutrition, etc. Even with as much as I know, I also know that If you want to be the best, you can't get there on your own. You need to surround yourself with great coaches. Everything is done so much more efficiently with great coaches. The coach is specializing in that one area and you often realize that you don't know as much as you think you did anyway.

Working with a mental coach can be a time-consuming process. You're adding a whole other element to the preparation of your fight. It's just like you would spend time in your gym lifting. You have to invest time weekly, daily or semi-daily basis doing your imagery exercise, speaking with your mental coach and re-affirming your green light thoughts and all of the things that you need to do. If you don't put in the time and effort into your training, it's not going to pay off for you on the night of the fight. Mental conditioning is like adding another aspect to your training.

Fighters and athletes need to look at mental conditioning as something that they do just like they do wrestling, training and weight conditioning. Most fighters think they need to work harder. What they need to do is work smarter.

Understand that there is a big mental component of fighting your best when it means the most. If you're like most athletes, it's about 90% physical, 10% mental in your preparation; yet, when that cage door shuts and it's just you and the other guy, it's about 90% mental, 10% physical because all of the training and all of the work is done.

# CHAPTER #1 REVIEW

- [ ] Training is physical, fighting is mental
- [ ] Confidence from physical work is key
- [ ] Training the relaxation response
- [ ] Always anxiety and self-doubt
- [ ] The butterflies never go away
- [ ] Control what you can control
- [ ] Other fighters should try mental conditioning
- [ ] Surround yourself with great coaches

## MATT CARPENTER, TCU HORNED FROG, CHANGES MENTALITY, CHANGES CAREER

*M*att Carpenter came off the bench for the St. Louis Cardinals in Game 3 of the 2012 Major League Baseball National League Championship Series and hit a home run to help lead the Cardinals to victory. I was fortunate to get to know Matt and have worked with him since his freshman year at Texas Christian University. Matt is a player who turned his career around by making a decision and then had the discipline to follow through with commitment on his decision.

*Many people make decisions to change how they live their life or approach various aspects of their daily routine. Few follow through on those decisions. Matt did and turned his career around and made himself a Major League player and one of the most influential and important players in TCU history.*

## BASEBALL IS IN HIS BLOOD

I played high school baseball in Texas at Elkins High School, and my father was my head coach. I was always a baseball junkie, a guy who lived, breathed and slept the game. It was in my blood. My goal was always to get to the Major Leagues. I was a student of the game like many kids who grow up around the ballpark.

I had a good high school career and was a highly recruited player. I ended up choosing TCU as my college of choice and when I got to college, like many freshman, I had a rude awakening. I was, for the first time in my life, in an environment where I was no longer the best player on the team. When you get to college baseball, everybody was the best player on their high school team.

I let myself get lost in the shuffle as a freshman for a few reasons, but mainly just because I really hadn't learned the skill of discipline that it takes to succeed at the higher levels. You can get by in high school if you have talent, but when talent starts to even out, it takes more than talent, it takes discipline, confidence and a relentless work ethic. Unfortunately for me, it took an injury, an eye-opening experience for me as a junior, to re-develop myself as both a player and, really, a person, and start putting those little daily disciplines and the mental game into a lifestyle. I started to actually implement the mental conditioning program and the things Brian Cain was teaching us at TCU into my life. From that point, it jump-started me onto the path I am on today as a professional athlete and Major League baseball player.

## INJURY IS AN EYE OPENER

I was always a guy that when I was at the field I worked hard. When we started to learn the mental game my freshman year when Cain came to TCU, I was a guy who always listened to what was being taught, and I was the guy that really, really wanted to be great but wasn't doing the things necessary to be great. When I was at the field or working out, I thought I was getting after it, but I never took that extra step.

My junior year, the first year to be eligible for the Major League baseball draft, I had Tommy John Surgery that season and took a medical redshirt. I watched guys that I had come to TCU with that were in the same classes with me getting drafted and going on to play professional baseball. They were living the dream that I think all college baseball players share.

We all kind of share that mentality that we want to go to a good college baseball program for three years and then get drafted into professional baseball. When that plan gets interrupted with an injury, you can get bitter or you can get better. When I got hurt and stepped away from the game, it opened my eyes.

I realized I had been sacrificing the gift I had been given to play this game and knew I needed to make some changes. I hit the gym and the nutrition table smarter and harder than I ever had before. A lot of guys didn't recognize me when they came back to campus that next fall.

**CAIN'S COACHING POINT:**
**What is something that has happened in your career or your life that made you open your eyes and change?**

_____

_____

## REDEDICATING YOURSELF IS NECESSARY

I ended up rededicating myself not only on the baseball field but also in other areas of my life: my nutrition, my off the field habits. I lost close to 50 pounds. I dedicated myself in the weight room and underwent almost a full makeover as a person both physically and mentally. That spring and summer, a rededication really helped jump-start me and propel me into the position that I'm in today.

## COLLEGE BASEBALL IS SPECIAL, ENJOY THE JOURNEY

I absolutely, without a doubt, am an advocate for college baseball. If you're a guy that's in high school and you're a borderline draft or college player and you're thinking about whether you want to go to college or sign professionally, I think it's a no-brainer.

The college baseball experience is something that not only developed me as a player, it developed me as a person, as a husband, as the man I am today. The life lessons that I was taught as a college baseball player were second-to-none. I would never take back that opportunity to gain those experiences I had in college. I think it's so critical and so valuable to becoming the player and person that you need to be to survive the temptations and pressures of professional baseball.

I see it all the time. Coming up through the Minor Leagues, a lot of the guys that were high school drafts were missing one of the most fun and best developmental parts of baseball which is playing at the college level.

I am not trying to take anything away from them because it's not like they are bad people. There are plenty of people who have gone on to be successful without going to college. But they're just missing that life experience that you get while you are in college and you are part of a college baseball program. All the relationships that I built being a college baseball player, I wouldn't trade those for anything.

**CAIN'S COACHING POINT:**
We often get so focused on the destination that we forget to enjoy the journey. What is the destination that has been pulling you out of enjoying the journey?

_____

_____

## LEARN TO ENJOY ADVERSITY

I have learned that adversity is a necessary part of the road to success. I have learned to like the struggles, even the struggles that I had in my first couple of years. My college coach, Jim Schlossnagle, recently asked me "If knowing what you know now, you could go back to your freshman year and do it all over again and make some better decisions, would you do it?"

As I thought about his question, and I have thought about it many times, I don't think I would. I think that the struggles and adversity I went through in my first couple years there and the changes that I ended up having to make have made me the person and player I am today. I would not be in the same position I am today if I would not have gone through that adversity and learned from those experiences. My nickname amongst my professional teammates is "The college hero: 'Matty College'." They're always giving me a hard time about it because I just love college baseball.

## TCU APPROACH WORKS
## IN PROFESSIONAL BASEBALL

At TCU we played with a relentless, positive energy. We played the game faster and harder than I had ever played it and harder and faster than I have seen it at the professional level. Coach Schlossnagle has a system that gets you to play with energy and enthusiasm and as a Minor League player, I really think if there was one thing that I could say that separated me from the other guys that I was competing with, it was that energy for the game and the will to win, not just on the scoreboard, but EVERY pitch.

## CORE VALUES BECOME WHO YOU ARE

At TCU, our core values were to be selfless, to be a great teammate and to put the team first and last, to play with great energy and attitude because the attitude you take is a decision you make and to commit to excellence in all you do because excellence is a lifestyle, not an event.

Coach Schlossnagle used to always say that there were two things that he would not coach: our attitude and effort. He said that if we did not have those two skills, we were never going to make it. The funny thing is, he is the best coach in the country in my opinion at coaching those two things. He models them.

**CAIN'S COACHING POINT:**
**What are the core values that you currently model and are they the values that you want to model? If not, what are you going to do differently today to model the person whom you want to become?**

_____

_____

## CARRY OVER TO PROFESSIONAL BASEBALL

It was hilarious to me because when I got to pro ball, playing with energy and having a will to win this pitch and having a daily routine were skills that I did not even have to think about, they were engrained in me from my days at TCU. Those were the two things that separated me the most from other guys and it was funny to me because I did not even think about those parts of the game. That was just the way I played; that is what college baseball and playing for Coach Schlossnagle did for me.

In the Minor Leagues, I was gaining attention from the St. Louis organization and separating myself from other guys just by the things that I didn't even think about doing.

## GREAT COACHES HELP MAKE GREAT PLAYERS & GREAT PLAYERS HELP TO MAKE GREAT COACHES

My dad used to always tell me that great players make great coaches. I think that it is a two way street. Great coaches also help make great players.

When I was at TCU I played for three guys that are now head coaches in big-time programs. Coach Schlossnagle is still at TCU and is the 2013 Team USA National Collegiate Team Field Manager, Todd Whitting is now the Head Coach at the University of Houston and Randy Mazey is now the Head Coach at The University of West Virginia.

What made them so great is that they would do anything to help you develop as a player. We brought in Brian Cain to work with us and did other great things as a program. They were always willing to go that extra step that not every program is willing to do. If there was anything that they thought would make us, even just a slight edge, like .1% of an edge, we did it. They as a staff were always willing to make that investment into our development.

**CAIN'S COACHING POINT:**
All professional athletes have coaches. They are the best athletes on the planet and they still have coaches. Who are your coaches and in what areas of your life do you want to find a coach who can help you take your game to the next level?

_____

_____

## HEAD COACH MUST SET A TONE

Coach Schlossnagle also set a tone for the program that we were going to get after it every day and come to the park with the mentality of, "We have this time to get better right now. Let's make the most of it."

I have never been around a guy who, literally, everything he does is centered around being a better coach, building a better program, making his team better and making his players around him better.

I remember him telling me in the recruiting process that he doesn't hunt, fish or play golf. His life centered around two things: his family and his baseball program.

I don't think he could've said that any better because it's the honest truth. Being in that environment with his influence for five years rubs off on you. You start to inherit those feelings yourself, you put them into your own style and system of how you live your life and you become like the people you associate with on a regular basis. They say that you are the average of the five people you hang out with most and luckily for me, one of those five people, for five years of my life, was Coach Schlossnagle.

## MENTAL GAME MATURATION

If I had to talk about what the mental game means to me, my answer would be different now than when I first got introduced to the mental game my first year of college. The first time Brian Cain came to work with us at TCU I had no clue what it was about and like most players, was skeptical at first.

I can honestly say that the mental game has changed my life. When you get to the point that I have gotten in my career, the mental game hits you like a ton of bricks. You realize that your biggest enemy and your toughest battle in baseball is yourself. I think it is that way at every level, and especially when you get to the big leagues.

Everybody in this game is really good at what they do when you get into professional and college baseball. What separates the guys who move from good to great and what separates a Minor Leaguer from a Major Leaguer, or even a college baseball player from a professional player is the mental game. There is no question in my mind.

**CAIN'S COACHING POINT:**
**What is something that you resisted or did not understand at an earlier age and now are a believer in and make a staple of your life? Why do you think it took you so long to learn this?**

_____

_____

## TALENT IS NEVER ENOUGH

There are plenty of guys I played with or against in high school and college that were, no doubt, better baseball players than me. They will admit it and so will I. The reason that I am still playing and they are not, from my perspective, is I had a better grasp of the mental game than they did.

There's just no doubt, in my mind, that the mental game is the biggest part of succeeding at the highest level. Being able to separate all the negative thinking and the red assassin, that voice inside of your head, all the red lights and the things that get in a player's way from being great. If you can become aware of when you start to beat yourself and develop techniques like breathing, routine and positive self-talk, final thoughts to control your mind while you're playing this game, you're going to give yourself the best chance to be successful.

## YOUR BIGGEST OPPONENT IS YOU

A staple of our mental game at TCU was to learn your red lights so you could release them and then refocus on the next pitch. A red light is a symbol for when you are out of control mentally, physically or emotionally and are not playing in the present. A yellow light is when you start to recognize it and a red light is when you have lost it.

A red light is when you make an error and you're starting to think about the past or future and your mind is racing. When you get to that red light mentality, that negative thought process causes you to get in your own way of being successful and you end up beating yourself.

A green light would be when you're feeling at your best, when there's nothing but confident, aggressive and routine self-talk and action. A green light means you are positive and thinking that you will make the play or are going to drive the pitch he throws you. In the green light mentality, positive thoughts are always flowing in your head.

When you are in red lights you start thinking negative. You've made an error or you've struck out and that voice in your head, the red assassin starts saying. "Man, I don't want to strike out again. I've already struck out once." Or, "Oh, man, this is the biggest game of my life. I'm in the playoffs. This is Game 3 of the NLCS, and I don't want to mess up, there are so many people watching, I hope I don't make a mistake on national TV." Those are the kind of thoughts that you want to stay away from, and that's what I mean by that red light mentality.

**CAIN'S COACHING POINT:**
**What are some ways in which you are your biggest opponent?**

_____

_____

## THE RED ASSASSIN ALWAYS SHOWS UP

The red lights are always going to be there. It takes a lot of practice to recognize your red lights and be able to release then and refocus back into the present moment.

The work that I put into the mental game at TCU, working with Brian Cain, was made of techniques that can help you to stay in the present, focused on the process with a positive mentality.

When the red assassin shows up, you have to release those mental bricks by being able to recognize when you're starting to think negatively and then have a release to go to that helps you to get yourself out of it. Everybody has their own mental game system of how they release their red lights.

I use a focal point and a deep breath. Some hitters use their batting gloves or the foul pole as a focal point. I don't actually wear batting gloves so I had to come up with something else to help me regain my focus.

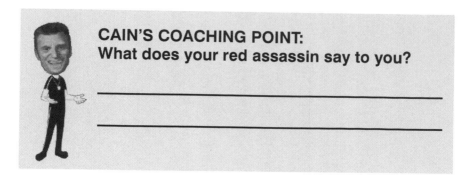

**CAIN'S COACHING POINT:**
What does your red assassin say to you?

_____

_____

## DEEP BREATH SLOWS THE GAME DOWN

When I start to feel like my mind is racing and I'm thinking negative, that's when I really try to control my breathing. One of the things that I learned early on in my career is that a good breath is a very vital tool in slowing the game down. And we talk about slowing the game down every day at the Major League level. I think that's a huge part about baseball.

That is really the key to the mental game of baseball, your ability to slow it down when things speed up. The breath is the deep, cleansing release of nervous energy that helps you to stay locked into the present and to winning this pitch. I take a breath before every pitch at the plate and on defense.

## MENTAL IMAGERY IS IMPORTANT

I also use mental imagery and visualize as I take my breath. As I am inhaling, I see what it is in my mind that I want to do with my body and then when I release that breath and exhale, I am literally releasing all those nervous butterflies or whatever negative feelings I have. I'm just releasing it out of my mouth and visualizing it coming pouring out as I exhale. That mental image helps calm me down and puts me right back in that mindset that I need to be successful.

## FOCAL POINTS ARE HELPFUL

My focal point has always been my cleats. If you watch me hit, you will see me look down as I step in the box and what I am doing is looking down at my cleats. I know that is my focal point that I can look at and realize, it's time to go to work and win this pitch. My focal point helps me to get back in that good frame of mind, focusing on the things that I can control and letting go of the things I can't control. The focal point helps me to stay in the present moment and take it one pitch at a time.

## PLAYING ONE PITCH AT A TIME

Playing one pitch at a time is being focused exactly on what is happening in the present, what is going on right now. If you are still thinking about your previous at-bat or the error that you made in the first inning, you are not fully focused on what's happening right now.

You are going to be either a step late on a ground ball hit to your left, be in the wrong position on a double-play or not be able to cover the defensive ground you normally can. You are going to be a step off because you are not focused on this present moment.

As a younger player, I really had no grasp of what it meant to play one pitch at a time or how to do it. I think a lot of guys go through that in their career where they are just not aware that you can train and develop your ability to play one pitch at a time.

Recognizing when you get out of the present is one of the key ways to be able to get yourself back into the present. Everyone wants to be the best player they can be and live up to their potential. With that strong desire often comes the trap of constantly thinking about your last at-bat and how you could've made it better or if, in your first at-bat, you strike out or take a pitch you should drive, you think about that event like it is life and death. You over-analyze every aspect of the game because you think that is the way you should be thinking because you want to improve.

The reality is that you are just getting in your own way and over-analyzing everything only helps you to beat yourself. Recognizing that I was getting in my own way and that my current thought process was only going to make this game get even worse if I continue to think like that was something I had to learn. I had to learn that as soon as this pitch is over, it is over. You've got to flush it.

## FLUSH IT

I will actually use mental imagery of flushing a toilet and saying, "OK, that pitch or at-bat's over, nothing I can do but learn and move on." I think having a physical release that you use like taking a breath at your focal point or knocking the dirt off of your spikes to help you release the negative mental mindset is maybe the most important part of the mental game.

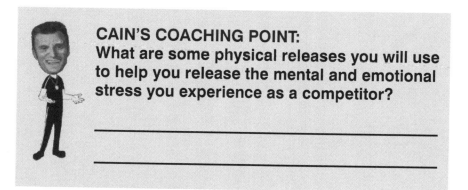

**CAIN'S COACHING POINT:**
**What are some physical releases you will use to help you release the mental and emotional stress you experience as a competitor?**

_____

_____

## YOU BEAT YOURSELF

You beat yourself more than the opponent beats you. You get in your own way. Your biggest enemy is always yourself. If you can get to the point where you can stay in control of yourself and the voice inside of your head, you will give yourself the best chance to be successful.

I always focus on 'this' pitch because there is nothing I can do about the last one. If I made an error the pitch before, it's over with – I can't change it. I've got to be focused on the next pitch. And if I'm locked in for an entire game on one pitch at a time, each pitch is its own game, then I'm going to give myself the best chance to play consistently at the level I want to.

## CONTROL WHAT YOU CAN CONTROL

I am a big believer in focusing only on what you can control and letting go of what you can't. For the first time in my career, this aspect of the mental game really jumped out at me. I saw how important a mindset of focusing on what you can control really is.

In 2012, for the first time in my life, I was a bench player. I was a utility player that no matter how well I did I was most likely going to come back to the park the next day and not be in the line-up. I could go to the park one day and get a start in left field and go 4 for 4 with two home runs and 5 RBI's. I could come back the very next day and not be in the line-up. For me, this was really hard from a mental standpoint because you want to play so badly, and you feel like you deserve to play, and you want to be in there. But, as well as you do, you have no control over writing the line-up.

The only thing that I could do is come to the park every day, ready to play, be focused on being ready to play. And if I was in the line-up then I could go out and give it my best effort. Early on in the season, I was letting this get to me. And it was causing me a lot of stress, and really affecting my play when I did get my opportunity to get in there.

Once I finally recognized it and accepted it, I released it, let it go and was able to play my best when I got my opportunities. Because of the work that I do in the mental game and the tools that I have, I was able to recognize this red light early and address it before it got too big and crushed my season.

It ended up being a strength of mine. I had to really get back to the basics and realize that I could not control the way the line-up was going to be written. I couldn't control if I was going to be playing or not. All I could control is that when I do get my chance to play, I play one pitch at a time and give my best effort every pitch. Those are the things that I can control.

If you are in the line-up every day, you can't control what the strike zone's going to be like, you can't control the weather or the field conditions. You can't control whether a family member just got sick or if you had a flat tire on the way to the park. Whatever the adversity, it will always be there. Life is a continuous series of problem solving events and once you realize that, you will not be so surprised when you have to compensate and adjust to get it done.

There are just too many factors in baseball and in life that you cannot control. You will either control what you can control or the game will control you. You can let the things you cannot control either have an impact on the way you're thinking that day or you can let them go and focus on what you can control: your attitude, your performance and your effort.

**CAIN'S COACHING POINT:**
**What are the main factors in your life that you cannot control that you try to and end up bringing more stress into your life as a result of focusing on what you cannot control?**

_____

_____

## HEARING AND LISTENING

Like many baseball players, I think when I was in my freshman and sophomore years of college, I was hearing everything that was being taught about the mental game, I just don't think I was listening until my junior year. What I mean by that is I always was in the meetings, was fired-up, ready to learn and I say "hearing" because as soon as our mental conditioning sessions were over I was back to doing what I did before.

My junior year came, and I finally listened and applied what was being taught. It took me three years to be ready to listen. I think that is true for a lot of players. As you get older, have more experiences and see how mental the game really is, you realize that the mental game is a way of life, not just something you do at home plate before each pitch.

The mental game is a lifestyle, not an event, and I used to think I could turn it on at baseball and kind of coast in other aspects. I thought I could use the mental game at the field and never thought about applying it to my life.

## THE MENTAL GAME OF LIFE

Once I started to apply the mental game on a daily basis in my whole life and not just at the field, that is when I started to make the most progress. The mental game principles that we are talking about can be applied to all facets of your life, and that was something that I started my junior year and continue to do to this day. This helped me, not only as a baseball player but as a person, because adversity doesn't just exist in baseball, adversity is everywhere in life. You can't control things in this life that happen every day. There are only certain things you can control. And if you can do those to the best of your ability, regardless of what it is, that is the process for being successful in life, not just baseball.

Getting injured my junior year was, I thought at the time, the worst thing that ever happened to me, and in hindsight it was the best thing that ever happened to me. It was a life-changing, sad reality that I had to go through, sitting out that entire year and just watching people grow up in front of me, leave and go on to play professional baseball. That was the moment for me when I decided that the mental game was going to be a way of life for me and I can look back now and say that I couldn't be happier for that whole experience.

## INEXPENSIVE EXPERIENCE FOR YOU

If I have one piece of advice for a competitor, and it really wouldn't matter what age it would be, it is that the quicker you can learn the mental game the better your career and life will be.

As an athlete, your physical tools will only take you so far. As good as you are physically, that may be as good as you are going to be. For some, that may be good enough to *play* at the Major League level, but they never make it. If you want to take your performance to the next level, if you want be an overachiever, better than the guys that you play with, that guy that people go back and say, 'How did that guy make it? I was a better player than he was.' The mental game is something you've got to buy into. I'm the living example of that.

There are plenty of guys that I've played with in high school and college, and in the Minor Leagues that are better baseball players than I am. I reached a higher level than they did because of the mental game, because I made it a lifestyle and used what I learned from Brian Cain, Jim Schlossnagle and TCU on a daily basis. If you really want to be excellent, get the most out of your ability and have no regrets when it comes time to take off your spikes, you will do the same.

If you do not currently believe in the mental game, maybe you will get lucky and you will have that eye-opening experience I did when I got hurt. You will see how important the mental game really is and you will change.

Follow Matt Carpenter on Twitter at @mattcarp13.

# CHAPTER #2 REVIEW

- [ ] Baseball is in his blood
- [ ] Injury is an eye-opener
- [ ] Rededicating yourself is necessary
- [ ] College baseball is special, enjoy the journey
- [ ] Learn to enjoy adversity
- [ ] TCU approach works in professional baseball
- [ ] Core values become who you are
- [ ] Carry over to professional baseball
- [ ] Great coaches help make great players & great players help to make great coaches
- [ ] Head coach must set a tone
- [ ] Mental game maturation
- [ ] Talent is never enough
- [ ] Your biggest opponent is you
- [ ] The red assassin always shows up
- [ ] Deep breath slows the game down
- [ ] Mental imagery is important
- [ ] Focal points are helpful
- [ ] Playing one pitch at a time
- [ ] Flush it
- [ ] You beat yourself
- [ ] Control what you can control
- [ ] Hearing and listening
- [ ] The mental game of life
- [ ] Inexpensive experience for you

# CHAPTER #3

## CASEY WEATHERS, MLB FIRST ROUND PICK, OLYMPIC MEDALIST & EMBRACER OF ADVERSITY

*C*asey Weathers was a first round pick, 7*th* overall by the Colorado Rockies in the 2007 Major League Baseball Draft and a 2008 Team USA Olympic Bronze Medalist. Weathers is currently playing in the Chicago Cubs minor league system.

## TEAM USA EXPERIENCE HELPFUL IN DEVELOPMENT

Playing for the Team USA Collegiate National Team in 2006 and the Olympics team in 2008 was amazing. They were opportunities that I was so excited to have and as I look at my baseball career, they are some of the most rewarding experiences I have had in the game.

My advice for anyone who gets to play for their country is to enjoy the experience and the competition. International competition is often a different level of competition. I was definitely nervous putting on the stars and stripes of Team USA and there will be a time where the game will speed up on you.

There can be added pressure because not only are you trying to perform well for your team and yourself, but you are representing your country. It's a really different opportunity when that Team USA is on your chest. The best players I have played with on those teams understand the nervous energy that comes with playing for your country and are able to use their mental game to best handle those emotions.

## OLYMPIC DREAMS BECOME A REALITY

To have the chance to go to the Olympics in 2008 was a dream come true and a once in a lifetime experience that I am very honored to have lived. As a competitor, you want to try your sport against the best in the World. It is really humbling to have an Olympic medal; it was an amazing experience. Very, very few people have that opportunity, and I was honored to be able to do that and just compete at that level. To put on that USA hat and wear the colors of your country and represent something that's so much bigger than you is amazing.

## MENTAL CONDITIONING IS A JOURNEY

I really started working on my mental game in 2007 when Tim Corbin, the head coach at Vanderbilt, brought Brian Cain in to work with us. I think the most important thing I have learned is how to build your confidence off of the process over results and how to slow the game down when it speeds up on you and deal with the pressure or self-induced anxiety that all athletes feel when they get onto that bigger stage.

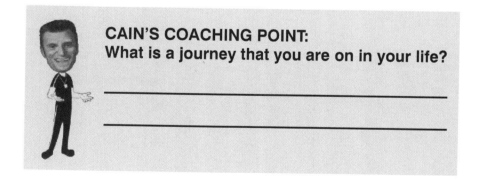

**CAIN'S COACHING POINT:**
**What is a journey that you are on in your life?**

_____

_____

## PROCESS IS EVERYTHING

To me the process is everything. I have been through some successful periods in my career, and I have been through some really down periods in my career. Recently, my game results have not been where I want them to be or where I think they should and will be and it's something that I have really had to deal with.

Regardless of my success or lack there-of, my approach every single day to do what I need to do to prepare doesn't change. I take my confidence from my preparation and process: from the pitches I make, not the results of those pitches. Regardless of my success or lack there-of, I come to the field the next day the same way. I don't come with my head down after a poor performance or my head up after a great performance. I come to work, and I come to do the same thing every day. I trust that my preparation routine and preparation process are going to get me the results I am looking for.

## CONFIDENCE IS A CHOICE

Another key for my mental game is to remember that confidence is a choice. I try to always stay confident and to not let my confidence go one way or the other depending on my results. I show up and get the work done each day that I need to in order to prepare. I have learned that success in baseball is about controlling the grind and establishing a successful routine and day-to-day mentality.

Taking the season one step at a time, one pitch at a time, 200feet a time, however you want to say it, that's how I try to compete in baseball and live my list. You have got to show up each day with a fire for that day and not worry about what you did before. Focus on what you are trying to accomplish right now. WIN – What's important now?

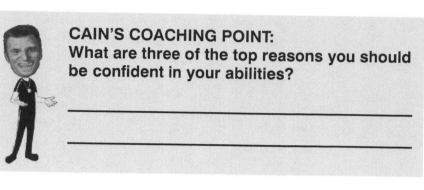

**CAIN'S COACHING POINT:**
What are three of the top reasons you should
be confident in your abilities?

_____

_____

## ROUTINES ARE KEY TO CONSISTENCY

Everyone has a different routine and you have to work to find one that works for you. Personally, I get to the field an hour before report time every day, no matter what the situation is. I don't feel like I am on time unless I am an hour early. I show up an hour early, get dressed, get my treatment in the athletic training room, take the same vitamin C supplement every day and drink a bottle of water. My routine when I show up to the yard each day doesn't change; it is the same every day.

If you do the same things every day to prepare, you are going to eliminate a lot of the outside factors and distractions. You're consistently being who you want to be every day.

I then do my early tubing and arm care exercise, do some early stretching, and then we head out with the pitchers at our designated time. The routine for our group of pitchers is set for us in how we are going to stretch, run and throw. I've used the same 15 throws almost every day. Every single throw in the program to get warmed up is scripted.

I will then go and work on my specific drills for how I am doing at that point in the season. I do whatever drills I need to be working on and those will change periodically with feedback from my coaches and from video review. The first 15- to 20-throws are always dedicated to helping me loosen up.

After we throw, we do pitchers' fielding practice and then head to the locker room for a little bit and usually try to just relax for about an hour or forty minutes. I may do some mental imagery, I may play cards with my teammates or sit in my locker and read a book, read articles online or just something to take my mind off the game so I'm not just constantly beating myself down about what I need to do to get better. It is very easy as a professional athlete to get consumed by your sport, even if you have a mental release. I think you can get burned out too quickly.

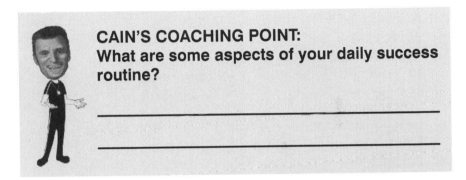

**CAIN'S COACHING POINT:**
**What are some aspects of your daily success routine?**

_____

_____

## MAKING THE SHIFT FROM THINKING TO TRUSTING

About thirty minutes before the game I will get in the shower and wash off that day's preparation and anything that I may be thinking about from my personal life. That's when I start moving from a thinking and preparing mindset to a trusting and competitive mindset.

I start getting my mind right for competition and mentally focusing on the game. I then get dressed and as I get dressed I put my uniform on the same way and then head out to the bullpen. In the bullpen I give myself time to relax for the first couple innings because I am usually not going in until any time after the 6th.

Once the 5th inning rolls around, that is when I'll start trying to stand up, stretch and do the same five- to six-stretches every time to make sure my legs are loose, just in case we get in a situation in the 6th and I get to go in. Typically, I have until the 7th or 8th, and I always start my routine after the 5th in case I need to go in there so I am fully prepared physically and mentally at anytime. I've already done the prep work.

## WHEN THE PHONE RINGS

When the phone rings in the bullpen and my name gets called, I go straight to the front of the mound and toss with the catcher until I feel like I'm loose. Then I get up behind the mound and do my crow hops down the mound until I feel loose. It doesn't really change. It's basically the same process every time the phone rings for me.

I throw to get loose and then depending on how the game situation works out, I'm throwing fastballs until my arm's hot. And then I'll start finding my location and will work the corners. I'll try to go in, in, out, out. And then I start working my sliders because those are the things you have to have in that order of importance when you get into the game: a good fastball, fastball command and good sliders.

When it is my time to go into the game, I give the ball to the catcher and I jog out. I jog the same way every time. I go straight to either third base or first base. I cut on the dugout side of the base, jump over the line. I run about halfway to the mound and then I walk to get the ball from the Manager. He says what he needs to say. And then I have the same pitching routine every time. Eight pitches: same eight every single time. Then I go through my pre-pitch routine.

I feel like all of that preparation gets me to a place where I am physically and mentally ready to compete and whether the results shake out the way I want them to or not, I will prepare the same way the next day. I feel like consistent preparation will lead to consistent results. I really trust my preparation process and feel that great things are going to happen for me.

## USING THE MENTAL GAME IN COMPETITION

After I have thrown my eight warm-up pitches, I use a very specific routine each pitch to keep me in the present moment. My routine consists of a deep breath on a focal point, a final thought for each pitch and a release if I get into red lights and the game starts speeding up on me.

I feel like if I do the same thing every time and can describe what I do as a process, I am giving myself the best chance to be successful.

Before every at-bat starts I am picking the smallest thing I can find to use as my focal point and take a breath. I use the left corner of the rubber and clean the dirt off of it so I can see the very, very corner tip of the rubber. I take three huge breaths – slow, low and controlled – into that smallest corner of the rubber. And I do that because the rubber's always there. I used to pick a rock on the mound, but that was too inconsistent. With using the pitching rubber it will always be there for me.

I take three big, deep breaths while looking at the corner of the rubber and then I'm ready to go and attack that hitter. I step on the rubber and then get another deep breath as I'm getting my sign and am trying to let all of the tension out of my shoulders. I come set and as I start towards the plate I use my pitch thought, which is usually "blow-it-up," "let it go" or "be free" because I tend to tense up a little bit and get over-excited when I compete.

## FINAL THOUGHTS

I really work to compete with a relaxed intensity and a controlled rage. I try to live in that one moment, that one pitch and my pitch thoughts are going to be based on what I feel most in the moment. I then just execute that one pitch and when I get the ball back from the catcher, I repeat the same process and attack the strike zone. After each pitch, I get right back on the rubber and don't waste any time. I take another huge, deep breath and as I'm exhaling, I pick up the sign from the catcher, come set, start towards the plate, final thought and repeat the process pitch to pitch unless I have a yellow or red light I need to release because I feel the game speeding up on me.

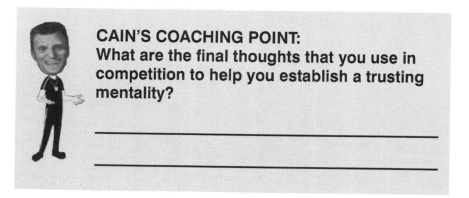

**CAIN'S COACHING POINT:**
**What are the final thoughts that you use in competition to help you establish a trusting mentality?**

_____

_____

## RECOGNIZE – RELEASE - REFOCUS

When I get into a red light, I get off the mound and go to the green grass to reset my mind and kind of clear my workspace. I go to the back of the mound on the grass, and I try to find a specific blade of grass or a piece of dirt on the mound to look at because when things are really going fast, you have to get back in control of yourself. You have to be in control of yourself before you can control where you are throwing the ball. If you lose control of yourself mentally, you lose control and your fine motor skills and performance suffer.

To release, I find that small rock, and once I calm myself down enough to pick up the rock, I take a deep breath and throw the rock away, which is symbolic of me releasing that pitch.

I then walk up back to the mound and the routine and process start all over again. That's my pitch-to-pitch routine and what I do to release if I get a red or yellow light on the mound. Recognizing my signal lights is something that I constantly battle with. I'm not perfect at the mental game, nobody is. Everyone gets red lights. You must take pride in your self-control and living in the present pitch to pitch. I'm always working on it.

After the game I will go back over my outing and evaluate either in my mind, watching video or looking at a chart of my performance. I will often look back and think that maybe I let the game speed up on me too much and know that I should have stopped and taken a deep breath. I should have gotten off the mound and taken care of my yellow lights before they turned red and I got to the point of no return. Recognizing my signal lights is something I am constantly working on and trying to be better at recognizing in the moment and the heat of the battle. The key is to always remain in control of yourself regardless of the competitive circumstances. There are very few things you can control when out on that diamond and the most important thing you can control is yourself.

## KEEP YOUR FOCUS ON WHAT YOU CAN CONTROL

As a baseball player and human being, you must have control of yourself before you can control your performance. A lot of times, players at the collegiate and professional level can beat themselves by focusing on things that are outside of their control. The things that are outside of your control are like fish hooks that will rip you out of the present if you are not aware enough to recognize and release them.

I see it all the time in the minor leagues, especially with the younger and less experienced guys. They will say stuff like, "Man, I threw a great slider and the guy hit it. I shouldn't have thrown that slider." I will then remind them that if you throw the pitch you wanted to throw where you wanted to throw it, it was a great pitch. The result was not what you wanted, but the process was executed with excellence. You may have thrown the wrong pitch strategically for the situation or you may have to tip your cap to the hitter who hit your best pitch.

If you do everything that you can within your control to throw the ball where you wanted it to go, that makes you successful. I think the younger guys have a hard time with understanding that you should evaluate your success based on the process, not the end result. Your goal must be in your control and you must be very clear on what you can and cannot control.

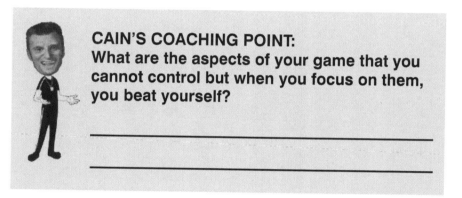

**CAIN'S COACHING POINT:**
**What are the aspects of your game that you cannot control but when you focus on them, you beat yourself?**

_____

_____

## RESPOND-ABILITY

The best pitchers understand that they choose their respond-ability in all situations. The less mentally mature guys get pissed off after the third baseman made an error, and as a result they gave up four consecutive doubles and end up allowing three runs. What they fail to realize is that you make your own momentum and momentum lies pitch to pitch. The error that the third baseman made had nothing to do with the next four hitters that hit doubles off of you. You still had to come back and execute quality pitches.

You can't control the errorless play of your third baseman. He made an error, he is human. That's baseball. That's life. It's going to happen. What happened after that is what is important. How you respond to the adversity. You can get bitter or you can get better.

## YOU CAN ONLY DO WHAT YOU CAN DO

Players would be much better if they could understand that they can only control where they throw the baseball. You can only do what you can do. You really have to put your focus on controlling yourself and doing your best to make quality pitches. That's really all you can do. Once that ball leaves your hand there's nothing you can do.

You must have a routine and be systematic and process-oriented in focusing on the things that you can do that are going to help you be able to throw the ball where you want to throw it. Everything else outside of that, the result that happens once it leaves your hand – organizational moves, umpires calls, plays made behind you by the defense. All that stuff is outside of your control.

## ORGANIZATIONAL MOVES

If there was one thing that I see negatively impact minor league baseball players that is out of their control, it is the overwhelming concern with organizational moves. As players, it is wasted time and energy to even talk about it. You can do nothing about what the organization does. You can best affect what they do by making consistent quality pitches and performing at your best on a consistent basis which is a by-product of preparing the best you can. If you play your best, hopefully the organizational moves take care of themselves, but you can't force it. That's going to happen or it won't. You, literally, have no control over organizational moves.

**CAIN'S COACHING POINT:**
What are the "organizational moves" that you think about that you can't control that pull you out of the present moment?

_____

_____

## ONGOING PROCESS OF SELF DISCOVERY

I have been grinding on the mental game now since 2007 and I am still not perfect all the time in my thought process out there on the mound. I death-grip pitches, I try to make perfect pitches. I understand that I do those things, and the mental game does help me with having an increased awareness and recognizing what I am thinking. I am better able to get back in green lights as quick as possible.

When on the mound, I try to be as relaxed as possible because when I get into yellow or red lights I tense up and try too hard to be perfect, but I understand that about myself. When I fall into that perfect pitching mentality vs. pitching with aggression and forcing contact, the mental game work I have done helps me to check in just a little bit faster and make an adjustment pitch to pitch instead of hitter to hitter or outing to outing.

I recognize I am in a yellow or red light and I go back to my release routine quickly. I look at that rock, take a breath and remind myself of my final thought, which is to be free and easy. I remind myself of my one and only goal: to make a quality pitch. I then am able to trust my preparation and trust that my body knows what to do, if I just let it.

## KNOW YOUR MENTAL ASSASSINS

We all have that little voice inside of our head, that voice of self-talk that we call the "mental assassin." There are two of them: the red assassin and the green assassin. You can tell when the red assassin shows up because he will start telling you that you are not good enough, that you can't do it, that the hitter is really good etc. When the green assassin shows up you can tell because he is positive and telling you that you can do it and that all you need to do is make a pitch.

Self-talk goes both ways. I have learned to embrace that voice when things are going well and release when the red assassin shows up and I start doubting myself or over-analyzing what's going on. When that negative doubt starts creeping into your mind, you must be aware and shift your self-talk. You have to kind of shift your perspective into thinking about what you want, not what you're trying to avoid.

## RECOGNIZING ASSASSINS CAN BE HARD AT TIMES

Recognizing that voice inside your head can be difficult because when you are competing and you get that adrenaline pumping, you want to go faster and harder. What you need to do is harness that adrenaline by taking your deep breaths and slowing your thought process down.

If your mind starts racing a little bit and your self-talk is negative, i.e. "Don't do 'this.' Don't do 'that.'", it can be hard to recognize that you are thinking this way in the moment. So you shift your self-talk and start focusing on what you want to do and what you are trying to accomplish.

There is always going to be a battle royale going on in your mind between the assassins. Try not to judge or beat yourself up, just know that the red assassin will always show up. Recognize it and release it. Embrace the confidence and the positives, when things are going well and let go of the negative when it shows up. Don't try to fight it. Just shift the line of thinking into something positive.

---

**CAIN'S COACHING POINT:**
**What do your green and red assassins say to you in performance that help you to recognize which one is speaking to you?**

**GREEN ASSASSIN**

_____

_____

**RED ASSASSIN**

_____

_____

---

## NEGATIVE ALWAYS LURKS IN THE WEEDS

That negative voice is always going to be there. It lurks in the weeds waiting to strike when you are at your most vulnerable point. Rather than beat yourself up for being negative, which just makes you more negative and makes it worse, accept the fact that those thoughts are going to come and then let them pass and focus more on what you want to do, not what you're trying to avoid.

## ESPN SCORE TICKER IN YOUR HEAD

The analogy I often use is it's like you're watching ESPN. And if you're sitting in the clubhouse watching ESPN, all the scores are going around on the ticker on the bottom of the screen. There's a bunch of soccer scores and hockey scores and basketball scores scrolling through. All of a sudden the Vanderbilt basketball score comes on the screen and I lock in and focus on that score because I went there. After that score goes by, I space out.

It is very similar to what it's like thought-watching when you're on the mound. All of these thoughts are going through your mind and the one that you lock in on, the ones that you watch, like I did the Vanderbilt score, are going to be the ones that manifest in your performance. If you lock in on the wrong score, per se, you're watching the negative thought, you're going to end up beating yourself. So, you've just got to be aware of what's scrolling across that mental ticker and lock in on only the thoughts you want to keep, and stick with those thoughts that are going to help your performance.

## THOUGHTS BECOME THINGS

Thoughts become things, I truly believe that. Not just in baseball, but in life. When you focus on positive things and positive thoughts, positive results will come your way. Maybe not in the immediate moment, but over the long haul, the marathon of the season, positive thinking is going to manifest in positive results. Unfortunately, negative thinking will also manifest in negative thoughts. Be careful of the thoughts you watch and the ones you let pass.

## HIGHLIGHT VIDEOS & MENTAL IMAGERY

I have a lot of positive videos that I watch. Videos of me from my days at Vanderbilt and the Olympics. Video of when I was throwing the ball really well. I watch that video a lot and always go back to it because I know that's who I am. That's who I can be. That's who I want to be. The guy in the highest pressure situations, fighting for that ultimate team goal, playing for an Olympic medal and facing the top competition from the around the world. The guy who carries himself with confidence, throws aggressive strikes, and putts the ball where he wants to.

The beautiful thing about video is that because I've seen it so many times, I can feel those positive images when I see them and even as I talk about the video I have those images just rushing through my head right now.

I often have trouble visualizing myself pitching the way I want to so I use that video before I do my mental imagery sessions to help me bring back the images of me pitching my best. I use mental imagery as part of my routine. I do it a lot in the shower before the game when I am kind of washing away that first half of the day, and getting ready to lock into being the pitcher I need to be to be successful.

The brain does not tell the difference between what you vividly imagine and what you physically experience. The brain processes those two experiences with the same psycho neuromuscular pathways.

Just by thinking about the things that you have done positively in the past, you're getting those feelings and neurons firing in your body. Essentially, you are creating the blueprint for your peak performance. The mistake a lot of players make is they focus too much on what they don't do well and not enough on what they do well.

Let go of the guy who hit a double off of you because you left the ball up and focus on the two or three guys you got out. Replay the quality pitches that you made in your mind over and over again like you are watching a highlight video. If you reply the time when you struck out the dude on three pitches, outside corner, outside corner, slider down, see you later. How are you feeling? How is your confidence? And all that kind of bubbles up to the surface, and now you take that out there with you to the game. And it's only positive.

## ADVICE FOR COACHES AND PLAYERS

My advice for players and coaches would be to realize that the mental game is bigger than just baseball. It is a lifestyle, not just something you do in sports. It will help you to get results, and if you truly understand what the Mental Game is trying to accomplish, which is living in the moment, you will get the most out of your abilities.

Achieving your true potential, that's the ultimate goal of the Mental Game. It's not my results on the baseball field that are most important in my life. Baseball is what I do, it is not who I am. What the mental game has helped me to do is be a better person and subsequently a better husband, a better son and a better player. And living in the moment, coming to work with a plan and a routine, understanding what I need to do to prepare every day, that's all part of the mental game. It's all part of what helps me get done what I need to get done every day to be the best I am capable of becoming.

## ADVICE TO THE WEARY

My advice to those who are weary of or uninformed about the mental game, or think that it is for the mentally weak: you are missing the big picture. The mental game gives you a way to live your life and it translates to the field as well. I take pride in coming to work consistently with the same work ethic and the same positive attitude every day.

## COMPARED TO WHAT

The mental game makes competing in baseball so much easier. It gives you a positive perspective and a 'compared to what' reference point that you can go back to so that you keep that attitude of gratitude and stay positive in a game of failure.

There are always going to be people that have it a lot more difficult than you. Compared to what they have gone through, you have it easy. Keep the joy of playing the game that you love.

Mental conditioning and commitment to excellence are really a lifestyle. They are not something you just do at baseball, but are a way that you live your life. This is how you get the most out of your potential. Whether you're playing baseball or when your career's done, if you go into real estate or back to medical school, whatever it is you do, the mental game is going to help you to be at your best on a consistent basis.

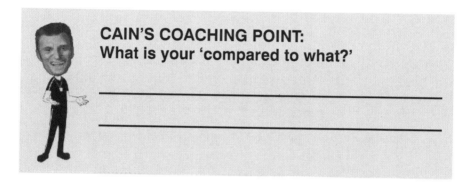

**CAIN'S COACHING POINT:**
**What is your 'compared to what?'**

_____

_____

You can follow Casey Weathers on twitter at @caseymweathers.

# CHAPTER #3 REVIEW

- ☐ Team USA experience helpful in development
- ☐ Olympic dreams become a reality
- ☐ Mental conditioning is a journey
- ☐ Process is everything
- ☐ Confidence is a choice
- ☐ Routines are key to consistency
- ☐ Making the shift from thinking to trusting
- ☐ When the phone rings
- ☐ Using the mental game in competition
- ☐ Final thoughts
- ☐ Recognize - release - refocus
- ☐ Keep your focus on what you can control
- ☐ Respond-ability
- ☐ You can only do what you can do
- ☐ Organizational moves
- ☐ Ongoing process of self-discovery
- ☐ Know your mental assassins
- ☐ Recognizing assassins can be hard at times
- ☐ Negative always lurks in the weeds
- ☐ ESPN score ticker in your head
- ☐ Thoughts become things
- ☐ Highlight videos & mental imagery
- ☐ Advice for coaches and players
- ☐ Advice to the weary
- ☐ Compared to what

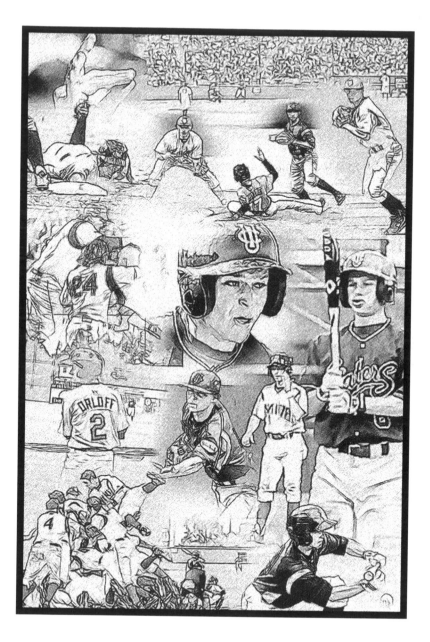

# CHAPTER #4

*B*en Orloff was an All-American baseball player at The University of California, Irvine (UCI) and impressed me with his work ethic and commitment to excellence from the first day I met him. Orloff led the Anteaters to their first College World Series and a #3 National Ranking in 2007. At the time of this interview he had recently finished the 2012 professional baseball season at the AA level with the Houston Astros organization. Orloff is a player that defines will-over-skill and excels at executing the fundamentals of the game.

## NOT HEAVILY RECRUITED OUT OF HIGH SCHOOL

I played baseball at Simi Valley High School in California and my junior year we won the State Championship at Dodger Stadium which still is one of the highlights of my career. I am undersized and was not heavily recruited by any schools at that point.

That summer after my junior year I was playing scout ball and started talking to a small number of schools. Then Sergio Brown, an assistant coach at UCI saw me play in a game where I played pretty well. The next day he sent me an email and said that he wanted to come back and watch me play again. I remember sending him an email back because no schools were really recruiting me and I said, "This is where I want to go school." And he said, "Oh. I'll come back and see you play one more time." And he came back and saw me.

He called me that night, and I went on an unofficial trip to UCI that next week out there and fell in love with Head Coach Dave Serrano and assistant coach Greg Bergeron and UCI as a campus.

67

I committed on that visit and loved going to school there. I learned a ton. I met Brian Cain in 2006, we went to the NCAA College World Series in 2007 and in 2008, we went to Louisiana State University (LSU) for a Super Regional, and were one inning away from going back to Omaha and lost.

## LOVES COLLEGE BASEBALL

I got drafted after my junior year but loved playing college baseball, loved UCI and wanted to get back to Omaha for the College World Series. My senior year in 2009, we were ranked #1 in the country for the majority of the year, hosted an NCAA Regional and got beat at home by Virginia, who ended up going to Ole Miss and winning the Super Regional there and went on to Omaha.

I was drafted in the 9th round by the Houston Astros, signed my first professional baseball contract and have just recently finished up the second half of the 2012 professional season in AA with the Corpus Christi Hooks.

**CAIN'S COACHING POINT:**
Knowing what you love about your sport will help you to embrace the grind that it takes to be successful. What do you love about your sport?

_____

_____

## WHAT IS THE MENTAL GAME

Baseball is a three hour game that can move really slow or very fast from pitch to pitch. The mental game is what allows you to really slow the game down and to perform at a consistent level.

The mental game is about having a routine to play pitch to pitch and not letting yourself get caught up in the moment. It is really about playing the game one pitch at a time. The mental game allows you to take what you do in practice every day and develop a trust so that in the game you can let your training, your preparation and routines take over so that you can trust yourself to play your game and not play scared to make mistakes or let the game start moving too fast. Trusting the work that you put in, all those hours of practice in the cage so that when it is game time, you can just go out and play and the situation or the moment is not going to be too big for you. You have prepared for it and are able to play it one pitch at a time.

## SLOWING THE GAME DOWN

Breathing is a big part of my mental game. Whenever I feel the game starting to go fast or in a big situation, I will take a good breath to get back into that relaxed state where I want to be playing the game one pitch at a time.

 **www.BrianCain.com/experience For BONUS Mental Conditioning Material & a video example of Ben Orloff's hitting routine from UCI.**

Slowing the game down is about being in control of your emotions. For me, taking a step back and really being aware of my breath and being able to take a good deep breath helps me to focus on the present moment and put all of my energy into that one pitch and not focus on anything else but being totally locked in for that pitch.

## BREATHING AND FOCAL POINTS – THE ROUTINE

When I am hitting, after I get my sign from the third base coach, I look at the label on my bat where it says Old Hickory and take a good deep breath, exhale and then step in the batter's box. I do that routine after every pitch and before I get back in the batter's box.

## DEFENSIVE ROUTINE

On defense, when I feel like I am speeding up I will look into my glove and get a good deep breath and bring my focus onto what I will do if I get the ball hit to me on this pitch. Part of my routine defensively is going through a mental routine in which I visualize and think about what I will do if the ball is hit to my left, right at me or to my right. By running through this in my mind before the pitch is thrown, I feel like I am more prepared to react when the ball is put in play.

## RECOGNIZING YOUR SIGNAL LIGHTS

When playing defense, I will notice when I get into a yellow light and then my mind starts to drift. Maybe it has been a long inning, there has been a pitching change and there are runners on base, and the ball has not been hit to me that inning. You can stand out there for 20 minutes and not touch the ball.

At that point, it is obviously a big situation because there are runners on base. That is when I can usually feel that my mind starts to wander. That's when I really lock in and take that deep breath, get back into my routine and into the green light before I get to red.

**CAIN'S COACHING POINT:**
**What is the number one signal you recognize that says you are in a red light and what says you are in a green light?**

**GREEN:**

_____

_____

**RED:**

_____

_____

## MENTAL IMAGERY

I use mental imagery as a part of my preparation process. When I am in the on-deck circle I like to visualize the pitcher and what pitch I am looking for and what pitch I think he is going to throw me. I then visualize myself doing what I want to do with that pitch. Mental imagery in the on-deck circle is huge for me. I really try to visualize my entire at-bat in the on-deck circle before I go hit.

## USING ALL THE SENSES IN IMAGERY

When I do imagery I try to make it as real as possible. I try to see the pitch and feel myself making contact with the ball and sometimes I even hear the ball hit the bat. I try to make it as real as possible. There have been times when I imagine myself getting a base hit in the right-center gap and it scores two runs. Then I go up to the plate and it happens exactly as I had imagined. I then stand at first base and just kind of laugh because I had just seen what had happened in my mind. It doesn't happen like that all that often, but when it does, it is pretty cool.

## CONTROLING THE CONTROLABLES

In baseball there are a lot of things you cannot control. You cannot control the umpires, the other team, the weather, etc. Your focus must stay on what you can control in the process. My mindset going to the plate and everyday is to control what I can control and let go of what I can't.

We can control playing with energy and focus. We can control our emotions, how we prepare, how we show up every day and how hard we play. *I think focusing on what you can control and letting go of what you can't is really a separator in professional baseball.*

The guys who are really good at the big-league level, over the course of 162 games, do a really good job of controlling their emotions, controlling their work ethic and not letting the factors outside of their control affect the way they play the game.

**CAIN'S COACHING POINT:**
**What are the aspects of your performance you can control?**

_____

_____

## GOING FROM COLLEGE TO PRO BALL

I think the biggest difference about professional baseball from the college game is that you are playing seven days a week. It is really important to be good at the mental game and being able to separate each at-bat and move onto the next pitch because when you're playing every night, the negativity can snowball on you if you let an 0 for 4 or one bad game negatively affect you or hurt your confidence. That one bad game can easily turn into a bad week if you let it.

It's really important to be in control of your emotions and not let the failure and frustration snowball on you and let it get out of control.

## ROUTINE IS CRITICAL

My routine is also a big part of my mental game. I will get to the field at the same time every day and I will do the same routine. When we play at home, I have a routine where I get to the field at the same time every day and do that same routine to make sure I am prepared and that I have time to do everything I want to do so that when it's game time, I know I'm prepared. I put all my work in as part of my pre-game routine and that allows me to just out and play.

When I was at UCI, I would always get to the field two hours before stretch, which was usually at 3:00pm. I would show up at 1:00pm and always brought my lunch with me. My routine was to eat my lunch, organize my locker, clean my shoes and just relax. At 1:45, I would go out to the batting cage and hit off the tee, hit some flips and work on some mechanical parts of my swing for about 20-25 minutes. Then I would go back into the clubhouse, relax, cool off a little bit and then start getting ready to go back out to stretch with my team.

Now, in professional baseball, I will get to the field for home games around 1:00-1:30 with my lunch, eat my lunch, go out to the cage, grab the hitting coach, work on some mechanical aspects of my swing for 20-30 minutes and then go back in the clubhouse, grab a little more food and just cool off until it's time to go out and stretch.

Preparation for me is huge because I think success is largely determined by how well we prepare ourselves. Anytime I am putting the hay in the barn, doing the work that I need to prepare for the game, I can go out and just play. I may still go 0 for 4 but that has nothing to do with my preparation. When that happens, I can still go home and put my head on the pillow, look myself in the mirror and know that it was just one of the those nights and that it wasn't because of a lack of preparation. I think that allows me to stay more consistent because whether I was 0 for 4 or 4 for 4, my routine the next day will be exactly the same.

**CAIN'S COACHING POINT:**
**What are the important parts of your routine that you do to keep you confident and trusting that you are prepared and ready to perform at your best?**

_____

_____

## SOME GUYS HAVE THE MENTAL GAME, SOME GUYS DON'T

It is very evident in professional baseball the guys that have a background in the mental game and the guys that don't. I see a lot of guys that will do everything right at the plate, make hard contact, line out, and when you try to give a guy a high-five he will throw a helmet or slam a bat and ultimately get down on himself when he did everything he could to succeed. He has not figured out that the result is outside of his control. Whether that at-bat resulted in a base hit or not is outside of his control.

When you look at a lot of the older guys who have played at the Major League level or have been around for a while, they all look the same after good and bad at-bats. They come back into the dugout, they put their helmet down, they put their batting gloves down, and they learn from their at-bat and then get into the next pitch with the team. When was the last time you saw Derek Jeter throw a bat or a helmet? He is the same all the time.

I think that for a lot of the younger players, you can see that frustration and the lack of success start building and building to the point where they lose confidence, start second guessing their preparation and their abilities and then all of sudden, one bad at-bat can turn into 25. The guys who have a grasp of the mental game can flush it and get to the next at-bat and get to the next pitch and one bad at-bat or one bad game doesn't affect them as much, nor does a successful game. You can slump just as easily by getting fooled by your success as you can by beating yourself up when it does not go well. It all comes down to consistency and consistency comes from routines and preparation.

## BATTING AVERAGE vs. QUALITY AT-BAT AVERAGE

Baseball is a game of failure. You can do everything right, get a good pitch, hit a line drive and not get the result, a base hit, that you want. You can do EVERYTHING RIGHT and still not get your result. It can drive you crazy, if you let it.

If you focus on batting average, which you cannot control, you are going to feel bad that you are 0 for 1 and are now hitting .273 instead of 274. If you commit to taking quality at-bats, over the course of 400 or 500 at-bats, your numbers are going to be there at the end.

 **www.BrianCain.com/experience For BONUS Mental Conditioning Material & examples of what a quality at-bat is.**

## WE OVER ME – TEAM OVER SELF

If you are focused on batting average, it becomes so much more about "me" and not about the team. You are trying to hit for your batting average because if you go 0 for 1 today, you are going to fall below .280, as opposed to just going out there today and grinding pitches and having quality at bats every time at the plate. I think if you stay focused on quality at-bats, being a tough out and playing one pitch at a time, the numbers are going to be where you want them to be at the end of the year.

## ADVICE FOR COACHES

The mental game is a huge difference maker. I saw the success that we had at UCI because of the mental game and I think if you are a college or high school coach and do not have a system for coaching the mental game, you are behind the times.

## WALK THE PLANK

I remember when Brian Cain came and talked to our team, he had a 4x4 plank that we all walked across as a way to cement our commitment to quality practice. We walked across the plank on the ground easily and then when it was 4 feet in the air, the game changed because we started to focus on what the outcome was vs. sticking with the process of going step by step and pitch by pitch.

That exercise really made me understand the importance of quality practice and that if we practice like we are going to play, then we can play like we practice and the game becomes a lot easier.

We competed harder in practice on most days than we did in games. When game time came we did not step up, we stepped back and relaxed, had fun and just played because we knew that we had been practicing at a high level and were totally prepared to play anyone in the country. I think that is how we won a regional at The University of Texas and a Super Regional at Wichita State, two difficult places to play, because we were totally focused on the process and on playing UCI baseball. The team in the other dugout was irrelevant to us. When we played Cal State Fullerton in Omaha it was the same. We just played the game.

We didn't have to be any better versus Fullerton in Omaha than we were all year. We trusted all that work we put in and when it was game-time, we just competed and had fun.

I think it is a huge thing for teams to understand that when you get into the post-season and the big atmospheres, don't try to do anything more than what you have done in practice for the last six months. Trust the process and know that if you go out and play well and have fun that you are going to be there in the end and have a chance to beat anybody.

In baseball, the best team never wins, it is always the team that plays the best and in 2007, we played our best baseball when it mattered most, the post-season.

## SPECIAL TEAM CHEMISTRY

The 2007 UCI team that went to Omaha and finished third was pretty special. We obviously had good players, but that team was all about the team. We cared for each other, we loved each other, we weren't selfish. We were all in it together and wanted to play well so we could win together.

The coaches were the same way. It was about the team. There was no "I" anywhere. We were competitive and fearless. We went to play at the University of Texas and UCI had never won a post-season game. We went in there confident and big. We were not going to be scared or intimidated by anybody because we knew that if we played well that we were going to have a chance to win and it was all about us. It wasn't about those guys on the other side of the field. It was about us. We were focused on trusting that we were prepared and were together and that was going to be enough.

It was a pretty special group of guys. It is five years later and the majority of us still talk on a regular basis. I think the mental game and our approach had a lot to do with that selflessness and commitment to something bigger than our individual selves.

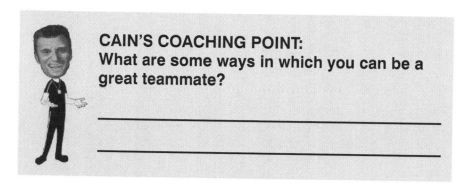

**CAIN'S COACHING POINT:**
**What are some ways in which you can be a great teammate?**

_____

_____

## OMAHA AND COLLEGE BASEBALL

College baseball was awesome for me. I wished that I could have had some more eligibility to play more than four years. It was awesome because it's all about the team and trying to get to Omaha.

You go to class, lunch, study hall, weights, social events and practice with these guys every day. It's all about the team. There was no ego on our team at UCI, where in professional baseball it can be a little different. Professional baseball, unfortunately, is more about the individual player that it is about the team.

Going to Omaha was just so special because growing up, I was a baseball crazy person and watched the College World Series every year. Getting to go there and play was amazing. I remember when we were busing there the day before our first practice and Coach Serrano had us all close our eyes and when we opened them we saw Rosenblatt Stadium, the Mecca of College Baseball.

I remember standing next to Sergio Brown in the dugout and he was telling me how he was "Standing right here in 1995 when Mark Kotsay hit his home run". It was amazing to feel the energy and all of the memories I had from watching TV of games at Rosenblatt, and to finally be there was just more than a dream come true.

## ADVICE FOR PLAYERS

The advice I would give to high school and college players is to control what you can control, develop a relentless work ethic, and play the game harder than other people think is necessary.

You don't want to leave anything out there to chance and you want to have no regrets when your career is over. When my career is over the one statement I want to be able to make is that I could not have worked any harder.

Put your work in to prepare and then when the game comes, be a great competitor, have fun: baseball is a kid's game. Play like you are in little league; enjoy the hell out of it.

There are a lot of players with great talent in this game, but you see just as many guys who are just average talent-wise and they've played this game for a long time. I think it's about being a great competitor, being a great teammate and having fun doing it because it's an awesome game. It's all about being a great competitor and being a great teammate today, because that is all you have control over. Yesterday is history, tomorrow is a mystery, today is a gift, that is why we call it the present, so don't count the days, make the days count and dominate the day, every day.

# CHAPTER #4 REVIEW

- [ ] Not heavily recruited out of high school
- [ ] Loves college baseball
- [ ] What is the mental game
- [ ] Slowing the game down
- [ ] Breathing and focal points – the routine
- [ ] Defensive routine
- [ ] Recognizing your signal lights
- [ ] Mental imagery
- [ ] Using all the senses in imagery
- [ ] Controlling the controllables
- [ ] Going from college to pro ball
- [ ] Routine is critical
- [ ] Some guys have the mental game
- [ ] Batting average vs. Quality at-bat average
- [ ] We over me – team over self
- [ ] Advice for coaches
- [ ] Walk the plank
- [ ] Special team chemistry
- [ ] Omaha and college baseball
- [ ] Advice for players

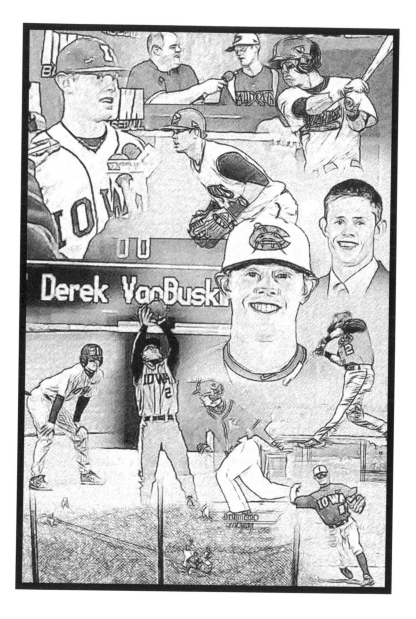

# CHAPTER #5

## JUSTIN TOOLE, IOWA BASEBALL PLAYER USES MENTAL GAME TO MAKE MOST OUT OF CAREER AND MAKE HISTORY BY PLAYING EVERY POSITION IN ONE PROFESSIONAL BASEBALL GAME

*Justin Toole graduated from Lewis Central High School in Council Bluffs, Iowa, in 2005. Toole was the Louisville Slugger Player of The Year for the state of Iowa in 2005 and also was named the Class 4A Bob Feller Pitcher of the Year. During his senior season he signed a scholarship to go play for The University of Iowa Hawkeyes.*

### COLLEGE BASEBALL IS A DIFFERENT LEVEL

My first year at Iowa, I really struggled. My sophomore year was the first year I was really introduced to the mental game and sport psychology. From that moment on, my career just kind of took off. I did really well my sophomore year, was named all-Big Ten and all-region as a second baseman, and carried that success into my junior season.

My junior year I was all-Big Ten and all-region again while recording the second most hits in Iowa's single season history, tying a school record with 5 hits in a game, and setting a new school record with a 25 game hitting streak, which was good for the 7th longest hitting streak in the nation in 2008. As a result of my strong season, heading into my senior year, I was named a pre-season All-American. I had made steady progress both physically and mentally and really felt like I had the right mindset, routines and perspective to play my best on a consistent basis. I was having another solid season and then in a game against Michigan State, around the end of April, I got hit by a pitch and broke my arm. At that point, my future and career got a little foggy. I wasn't sure if I'd have an opportunity to play again.

## PROFESSIONAL BASEBALL, WILL IT HAPPEN?

I always wanted an opportunity to play professional baseball. It always had been a goal, a dream of mine. I finally made it, but I had to take a wind-about road to get there after the injury. I wasn't completely healthy in time for the draft and, as a result, didn't get drafted. A couple of teams called on draft day, but I just had my cast off a few days before the draft and they wanted me to come, step in and play right away. I wasn't able to do that. I had to be honest with them and told them I wasn't quite ready to go.

Getting passed up in the draft was tough as growing up I always wanted to get drafted. I did hear from a couple teams in terms of free agency within the following weeks but nothing came of it.

**CAIN'S COACHING POINT:**
**Focus on the process, not the end result. If you want to be a professional baseball player and get drafted, focus on what you can do today to help you get 1% better. What can you do today?**

_____

_____

## DRAFT DOES NOT HAPPEN

After not getting drafted I was fortunate enough to sign on with an independent team for about a week and then got a phone call from the Cleveland Indians and signed my first professional affiliated baseball contract. I just finished my fourth season of professional baseball in 2012 and am absolutely loving the grind and playing the game. I am blessed to get the opportunity to play the game of baseball every day.

## BASEBALL PLAYER vs. POSITION PLAYER

I finished the 2012 season in high A, but I bounced around within AA and AAA for a while. I look at myself as a baseball player, not just a position player. I am a utility guy within the Indians organization, so wherever there's a need for a guy like me, I bounce around and do my job. I never know what position I will be playing when I show up to the park or if I will even finish the day with the same team I started it with.

**CAIN'S COACHING POINT:**
The next time a coach or person asks you what position you play, tell them that you will play anywhere you are needed to help the team win. You are a baseball player, not a pitcher or a shortstop. Then start to work at those different positions, especially if you are playing at a level below college baseball.

## PLAYS ALL NINE POSITIONS IN ONE GAME

At the end of August, my manager came up to me and asked if I wanted to play all nine positions in one game. Being a pitcher in high school and a little bit in college, I was familiar with being on the mound, and growing up as a coach's son, I was somewhat familiar with everywhere else. It was a no-brainer for me.

We won the game 4-2 and I played well. Being able to play anywhere is something that I take a lot of pride in as a utility player, being able to go out there and answer the bell when my number's called. I never thought I would play all nine in one game. It was a special night and something I'll never forget.

## MANAGING ROLE AS A UTILITY PLAYER

As a utility player, you show up to the field everyday and you don't know if you're going to be in the line-up or not. You don't know what position you're going to play or where you're going to be in the batting order. And in my situation, you might not know what team you're going be on tomorrow or you might not know what city you're going to be in the next day, so you have to be ready to go at all times. You have to be locked in as if you're playing every day, as if you're going to be the starter, as if you're going to go out there and be the lead-off guy or even the key guy off the bench.

## PRE-GAME ROUTINE ESSENTIAL TO CONSISTENCY

My pre-game routine starts right when I get to the field. I try to be one of the first guys to the field because I have access to the batting cages and the weight room. Getting there early, I don't have to work around anyone and can get in and get my stuff done. I don't have to worry about socializing and all that kind of stuff that a lot of guys like to do when they get to field. I like to get there early, get my work done and then kick back and relax a little before batting practice.

**CAIN'S COACHING POINT:**
**What are three things that you can do to start to build a pregame or pre-practice routine?**

_____

_____

I'm a very routine-oriented person. When it comes to getting in the cage, I like to do my tee work, one-hand drills, and a few other drills that get me in a good spot heading into the game. That way when I get into the game, I don't have to worry and I can trust my preparation and know I am ready to go and ready to compete.

For me, defense is the hardest in terms of being prepared because as a utility player, I play all of the four in-field positions as well as some outfield. It takes a lot of hard work during batting practice to make sure I get ground balls at second base, at third base, at shortstop and at first base. I take that part of the preparation process very seriously so that I can be ready for every situation because I never know where I might be playing.

After batting practice I always grab something to eat and take a quick shower before I get ready for the game. The shower for me is the thing that separates practice from the game. I know that after I shower, it's time for me to compete and not worry about anything else. I usually wear eye black when I play. Putting on the eye black is another thing I like to do that puts me in game mode.

I might not be in the line-up, and in the third inning someone pulls a hamstring or someone's arm is a little bit sore or someone gets hits by a pitch, and I get thrown into the fire and have to be ready for all those situations. I take a lot of pride in my pre-game routines so that when my name is called I am ready to go. My pre-game routines help me to be in the right spot mentally as well as physically.

 **www.BrianCain.com/experience**
**For BONUS Mental Conditioning Material &**
**your routine writing worksheet.**

## PLAYING ONE PITCH AT A TIME

Playing one pitch at a time is the toughest part of baseball because there are about 300 pitches in a game and that means about 300 games within the game. I approach each pitch like it is a new game. You also play every day of the week and play somewhere between 120-160 games in 130-170 days depending on what level of the minor leagues you are at. There are not a lot of off days. Playing one pitch at a time in the present moment is a challenge, but is the most essential part of the game.

I try and make it as simple as possible in the game. I have a routine where I run though my mind what I am going to do if the ball is hit to my right, left or center. I also make sure that I communicate with my teammates because when you talk you get yourself into the moment and get out of your own head.

At the plate, it's always the same thing for me. I have the same in-box routine for every pitch. When I walk to the batter's box, I take possession of it. I mess with the dirt, stomp around a little bit and make it mine. I do the same thing every single time I step to the plate.

I then get the sign from third base and then step in. A lot of people make comments from high school or college teams because when they come see me play or when I go back and workout in the off season, my routine is always the same. I have been doing it this way for the last eight or nine years. It is a routine that works for me and one that I've had a lot of success with.

## NOT THINKING ABOUT ROUTINE JUST WINNING THIS PITCH & GETTING PRESENT

When I go up to the box I'm not thinking, "OK, I've got to step with my right foot, I got to step with my left foot, I've got to tap the plate once." It's just something that has become ingrained in my memory. It's ingrained in me as a player. And that's definitely something that helps me out in terms of keeping a calm and confident mentally.

**CAIN'S COACHING POINT:**
If you win this pitch, and do it again, and again, the result will take care of itself. The routine helps you to stay focused on winning this pitch which results over time in winning the game.

## LEARN BY WATCHING

You can learn a lot by just watching your teammates and the game. I call it inexpensive and expensive experience. Inexpensive experience is what I can learn from watching my teammates while expensive experience is what I get from my own mistakes. Making it to major league baseball is about getting as much inexpensive experience as you can and speeding up the learning curve.

By watching the hitters ahead of me, I can tell what pitches are working for the pitcher we are facing. If you're hitting lower in the line-up, when you get up to the plate, you should feel like you have taken a few at-bats off of this pitcher already.

## INEXPENSIVE EXPERIENCE OFFERED

If I were to offer any inexpensive experience to players reading this it would be to make sure that you believe in yourself and your abilities. I have played at the highest level of the game, and I play with guys that are just as talented as guys that I played with in college that aren't playing any longer. In fact, I am playing with guys that are *not* as talented as people I played with in the past who are no longer playing.

Talent can only take you so far before the mental game is necessary to take you further. I am a firm believer that in everything that I have accomplished, I have beaten the odds. Non-drafted free agents do not stick around in professional baseball very long; they are usually just fillers for a few years. I have been able to turn my free agency into a four-year career and I do not plan on letting up any time soon.

**CAIN'S COACHING POINT:**
**My #1 piece of inexpensive experience is to control what you can control and take a breath each pitch. By breathing, you help slow the game down and stay in the present moment and if you focus on what you can control you make the game a lot easier.**

## PLAYING PAST ABILITY LEVEL

I have gotten further than probably my ability should have allowed me to because of my buying into the mental game. A lot of baseball players think they have to be perfect and they think that when you turn on ESPN and you see guys making amazing plays that those guys are superhuman and perfect. What I have learned is that they are not different, they are not perfect or superhuman, they are just like you and I. They are normal people just like everyone else. Everything is not easy for them, although they do make it look easy.

They work very hard, they don't go through the motions, and they also make a lot of mistakes. They deal with failure. They deal with struggle just like everyone else does. When I was younger, I always thought they were invincible and that they were perfect and didn't make mistakes. But being around the best players on the planet in spring training, getting to know a lot of the guys in the big leagues, I realize just how close the talent levels are all throughout professional baseball.

You don't need to put pressure on yourself to be better than you are, or try and be someone you aren't, or try to be perfect because nobody is perfect. Yes, some people are given extreme athletic ability, but just as many people play longer than you would think their ability should allow them to and a large part of that is their mental game.

## PERFECTION IS UNATTAINABLE

When I went to Iowa as a freshman, I went in and tried to be perfect. I went through that again when I signed with the Cleveland Indians. When I first came into professional baseball, I was trying to be perfect, trying to be mechanically right, trying to be mechanically perfect every time instead of just relaxing and playing the game. Perfection is unattainable. When you try to be perfect, you zap yourself of any trust in your ability and you go downhill fast.

A lot of players in college and high school baseball don't have a lot of struggles because they are naturally better than everyone else. When I got to Iowa, I played with and against everyone who was a stud in high school. That struggle my freshman year was one of the best things that happened to me because now, when I get myself in a bind or a jam, I realize struggle is an unavoidable part of the game and presents an opportunity to learn. I know that if I can battle through a struggle once, I can do it again.

You find out what you're made of when times are tough and when you struggle. My freshman year, when I struggled, I had to really dig down deep inside, figure out who I was as a player and as a person and when I figured that out and paired that with the mental game, everything just took off.

# RELAXATION IS A SKILL THAT MUST BE LEARNED

Being able to relax is a lot easier said than done when it comes to relaxing on the field. I was fortunate at the University of Iowa that our practices were very, very competitive. They put a lot of pressure on us in practice to succeed in certain situations. I was fortunate enough that my first year I struggled a lot and was stressed in practice every day. That competitive atmosphere in practice really allowed me, when I got into games, to learn how to relax. We practiced at such a fast pace that everything was moving faster than it does in the game. That allowed me to slow things down and be in the present moment during games.

Taking a deep breath was also a big part of helping me to relax. I will take a deep breath before each pitch both at the plate and in the field. I also use a lot of focal points, specific places on the field or in the stadium where I will look and take a deep breath to help calm myself down. Defensively, I constantly pick little pebbles out of the dirt and toss them in the grass as a part of my routine. If I can focus in on a pebble, then I can focus in on the ball when it's hit to me. Routine breathing, using focal points and picking up pebbles helps me to get into and stay in a comfort zone.

 **www.BrianCain.com/experience For BONUS Mental Conditioning Material & your free relaxation training audio tracks.**

# USING MUSIC AS A PART OF YOUR ROUTINE

When I struggle I often notice that I am not doing my routine and I can recognize this by my failing to breathe. My next step of mental recovery is to find focal points and pick up pebbles. I'm a very emotional, very hyper-active and intense kind of player and I learned in college that when I am on my way to the baseball field I cannot be listening to music that gets me all pumped up.

Maybe if I was playing football and had to sprint down the field and crush somebody, maybe I could listen to that. But playing baseball, that won't work for me as it is more of a relaxed game. I have turned into a big country music fan: kind of a more laid-back, slower kind of music guy. If I listen to something too fast and too crazy, it gets me too hyped up and I don't perform. I definitely use music as a way to get me locked in and to help me relax. It's different for everyone; you've just got to find what works for you.

**CAIN'S COACHING POINT:**
**You want to have two types of music on your iPod. Music that gets you dialed up and locked in and music that helps you to relax and dial it down. What are those two types of music that you have on your iPod?**

_____

_____

## MENTAL IMAGERY A BIG PART OF PROCESS

I am a big believer in the use of mental imagery. At Iowa we did a lot of mental imagery before games when we went over scouting reports on opposing pitchers. Having played for three years, I got to know the different pitchers in the Big Ten and when I faced them I had an idea of what their mechanics looked like so I could better mentally prepare to hit off of them.

It is eerie when you imagine things from a hitting standpoint such as getting pitches in a certain spot, taking a certain swing and driving the ball to a certain spot and then it happens exactly that way in a game. Numerous times in my career that has happened and I always laugh because I had seen that pitch and that play in my mind over and over before it ever happened on the field. When it happens, it is déjà vu. The more you can use mental imagery, the better it gets.

 **www.BrianCain.com/experience For BONUS Mental Conditioning Material & mental imagery audio training tracks.**

## POST GAME IMAGERY

After games, I will replay the game through my head. I will replay the good plays and good at-bats for the positive reinforcement and will replay the negative situations. For example, if I missed a couple pitches and struck out, or missed a ground ball, I will go over those mistakes a couple times and picture what I should have done better and see myself make the play.

Growing up, I did mental imagery all the time without really realizing what I was doing. I think a lot of players can relate to that. When you are a kid and are in the back yard, you are always putting yourself in bottom of the 9th, bases loaded, two outs in the World Series, trying to hit in the winning run or striking out the final batter. Growing up I would always put myself in those kinds of situations and I think I benefitted from doing that without really even knowing that I was using mental imagery. Once I got involved into the mental game, I just took my mental imagery to another level.

## CONTROL WHAT YOU CAN CONTROL

Controlling what you can control, especially from a hitting standpoint, is a huge part of mental toughness in baseball. All you can do is get a good pitch to hit and put a good swing on it. Once that ball leaves your bat the result is out of your control.

The umpire might make a bad call, the shortstop may make a diving play, you may hit the hardest ball of your life right at someone.

 **www.BrianCain.com/experience For BONUS Mental Conditioning Material & your list of the most common controllable and uncontrollable aspects of baseball.**

## BATTING AVERAGE IS SATAN

The hardest part in baseball is trying to let go of batting average and your statistics that get posted everyday because they are largely out of your control. I am guilty of focusing too much on results throughout my career just as many people are because baseball is a statistically-driven sport.

When you get out there the main thing you are trying to do is hit a line drive, hit a ball hard, move a runner over and get the job done. Being a situational hitting guy is a huge part of a team's success but never shows up in a stat book. When there's a runner on second base and no outs, move that guy over with a ground ball. When there's a runner at third base, hit a ground ball at second base and score that guy. That's what I think about going up to the plate, and a lot of my success as a player has come from being an unselfish situational hitter.

**CAIN'S COACHING POINT:**
The pitcher's version of a quality at-bat is executing a quality pitch. A quality pitch is throwing the ball where you intended to throw it.

Too many players focus on batting average (outside of your control) instead of quality at-bat average (inside of your control). I think at the lower levels of baseball, little league, summer ball, high school etc., a huge issue kids have is trying to get to the next level or trying to make all-star teams so they focus on stats. I can assure you that if you focus on quality at-bats, you hit the ball hard, you do your job as a hitter, moving runners over, and situational hitting, the batting average number will take care of itself.

**www.BrianCain.com/experience For BONUS Mental Conditioning Material & your list of the different ways you can have a quality at-bat in baseball.**

## IF YOU HIT THE BALL HARD, YOU HAVE GOOD STATS

In all my days of playing baseball, twenty something years, I have never been around a kid that hits the ball hard and didn't have success in terms of statistics. If you can think about hitting the ball hard, situational hitting and having quality at-bats, I can assure you that the numbers will take care of themselves.

## YOU DON'T HAVE A LOT OF CONTROL IN THIS GAME

When I first started playing professional baseball I used to struggle with not being in the lineup because I had always been a kid who had been in the lineup every day. I had to accept that unless you are the manager, you don't control whether you are in the lineup or not.

The higher up you go in baseball, the more competitive it gets. Just because you play well one day, that does not mean you will play the next. That happens in high school and college, but not in pro baseball. I had to remind myself that I can control my attitude, my perspective and effort. When you get a good grasp on what you can control and let go of what you can't, it makes it a lot easier to show up at the field every day. Just because your name's not in the line-up doesn't mean that you're not doing well. It may be a better match-up for your team, or maybe your coach feels that there's somebody else that is a little bit better against left-handed pitchers compared to right-handed pitchers or something like that. Once you get the "me, me, me" out of your head and you get more of a team mentality going, you will have a lot more success.

## WE OVER ME MENTALITY

In professional baseball and all throughout my career, I have played on some tremendous teams where it's not "me, me, me." It's all about the team. You don't see that often in pro baseball because it is really an individual sport. The championship teams where people put "we" and team success over the individual success are the most fun to play on. The teams that I have been on that have had a lot of success are the teams that are close together, the teams that play for each other. As a result of the team-focused mentality, we ended up having a lot of individual success as well.

**www.BrianCain.com/experience For BONUS Mental Conditioning Material & your official Brian Cain Peak Performance WE OVER ME sign of success.**

## FRIENDS AND COMPETITORS

A lot of my best friends are the guys that play the same position as I do because we spend so much time together. It is tough because you become good friends with the same guys you are competing with. It can be tough at times, but I have been fortunate. With the Indians, the last two years in spring training, my roommates have been released close to the end of spring training before we broke with our teams. Both times I had grown close to the guys after sharing a hotel room with them for a month, doing everything together, eating meals away from the field. Doing those things together, you get to know them a little bit more, things with their personal life, families, and girlfriend or wives.

One of my best friends in the Indians organization was a shortstop. We were roommates at spring training and he got released a few days before spring training ended. I am sure in the staff meetings it was him and me, and maybe a couple of other guys that were on the chopping block of names up for being released.

It can be hard going out there and competing against your friends. When one of your friends comes up and says, "Hey, I am done, I'm heading home," it is a tough thing to hear. At the same time you also have to realize it's a business, and you're out there to perform, and you are out there to do the best that you can. And when that time comes for a player, it's hard to comprehend and handle sometimes. But you do not know how long you are going to be able to play the game so you have to take advantage of it while you can.

In my senior year of college I broke my arm and I was not sure if I would ever play another pitch competitively. I was fortunate enough I turned that into four years of a professional career and do not anticipate stopping anytime soon, but I do realize that is out of my control so I focus on dominating each day the best that I can.

I have had the fortune of having friends that didn't let the game of baseball and the competition for the same position ruin the friendship. It can be hard when a good friend gets cut and one day you wake up in the same room as teammates and later that day they are gone. You realize that is part of the game and it can be hard, but you have to accept that someday you will get released and that you will not play forever. You just have to go to the field every day, work and focus on getting better at the things you can control.

## DIFFERENCE BETWEEN A FRIEND AND TEAMMATE

You have to keep it all about the team and being a good teammate. At Iowa, we reinforced there was a difference between a good friend and a good teammate. And sometimes, you do have to cross that line and be able to get in someone's face or tell someone, "Hey, you need to work a little bit harder." At the same time, you need to be able to look at yourself in the mirror if someone comes up and says, "Hey, you need to pick it up a little bit," or "You need to work on this. You need do that." Don't take offense to it, just realize that your teammates are trying to help you get better.

**CAIN'S COACHING POINT:**
What are situations in the past that you have let slide that you are going to address with your teammates?

_____

_____

## BE COACHABLE

You have to realize as an athlete that your teammates aren't coming at you thinking that you're a bad person, but they're coming at you thinking, "Hey, I want to win. I want you to help our team." Growing up, I had trouble with constructive criticism. I always thought people were attacking me. *Now I realize that you must accept constructive criticism as a compliment*.

When you get older and more mature you start to realize that people are not attacking you, they are actually looking out for you. When coaches and teammates stop giving you constructive criticism that's the point where you should start to worry. Coaches will always try and help a player who they feel has room for improvement. Never look at constructive criticism as a negative, look at it as a compliment.

## BASEBALL IS WHAT YOU DO, NOT WHO YOU ARE

There is a big psychological shift when you stop taking things personally and start taking them professionally. When you separate baseball being what you do versus baseball being who you are, you stop putting so much pressure on yourself and really start to enjoy the game.

When baseball is who you are, you put a lot of pressure on yourself, and you feel like you have to perform well or you're a failure. When baseball is what you do, it turns that pressure into pleasure because it's a game that you get to go out and play. There is a balance between taking the game really serious in your preparation but taking it not so seriously and having a little league, fun mentality when you compete because you know it's a challenge and it's supposed to be fun. And when you play and have fun versus making it a job, you always perform better.

Going back to my freshman year in college, I think that was something I struggled with. Baseball was who I was, not what I did. Going through those struggles, going through the failures, I failed to recognize that, "I'm blessed. I have an opportunity to play this game in college, blessed to have a scholarship to help to pay for some of my school."

Now, playing professionally I embrace that. I was a Carolina League All Star in 2011. That was really the first year where I can say I went in and played with the right mindset. A lot of times in professional baseball, you play not to get released instead of playing to make it to the big leagues. I feel like that was the first year of my career I didn't worry about the consequences of what might happen. I focused on what could happen if I went about things the right way.

**CAIN'S COACHING POINT:**
**Who are you outside of baseball or your sport. If you could never play the game again, what would you do with your life?**

_____

_____

## MENTAL GAME SHIFT CHANGES PERFORMANCE

The amazing thing was that in 2011 when I made the all-star team, it wasn't that my physical tools changed, I did not get tons better than the year before. My swing did not change a whole lot. What changed was my mental attitude and my approach to the field and how I showed up to the field every day.

I think it goes back to the power of the mental game. You can out-play your talent. *The best compliment I think someone can give me is that I play above what my talent level is and that I'm a ball player and play the game the right way*. Those are the two biggest compliments I think that someone can give me as a baseball player because you play above what your physical talent should make you capable of and you play the game the right way. I feel like at the end of the day, if you can say that about yourself, you shouldn't have any regrets and should know you left it all out on the field.

## TAKEAWAYS FROM TOOLE

The biggest thing that I think, with today's society, is there are a lot of people out there that'll tell you what you can't do, that you can't play "this" or you can't do "that." I was told in high school I wasn't good enough to play college baseball. I was told sometime in college that, "I don't know if you're good enough to play professionally." I used that as motivation.

## THINK YOU CAN

The one thing that I would tell coaches, is never tell a kid, "You can't do something." I'm a believer that if a kid feels like they can play college baseball, if they see it as a possibility, they will continue to work. *They might not be good enough YET, but if they think they can, they might; if they think they can't, they are right.*

If a kid wants to play baseball in college, I feel like there's a spot for that kid to play if he has the right attitude, if he works hard, if he goes about his business the right way, and is a learner.

## NEVER LISTEN TO THE DOUBTERS

As a player, never let someone tell you that you can't do something and discourage you from following your dreams. My dream, as an individual, was and still is to play major league baseball. I've accomplished part of that, I'm a professional baseball player, and I've even played in AAA, but I'm still trying to work my way up to the big leagues. Even If I don't ever make it to the big leagues, I'm not a failure because I didn't reach my ultimate goal.

## LEARN EVERYDAY

I am a winner because I am learning everyday and I am doing everything I possibly can to give myself the best chance for success in this game and to get to where I want to go. What I have learned from the journey has made me a champion regardless of whether I make it to the big leagues or not. Making it to the big leagues is my outcome goal. I focus on that 20% of the time, but 80% of the time I focus on today and doing everything I can to become the best player I can be.

Set your goals high for yourself and set the standards for your life high. Don't ever let anyone tell you can't do something. Work hard for it. But at the same time, if you don't quite get there, realize that you're not a failure or a loser. You must be a learner. *The only time you are a failure is when you quit and the only time you are a loser is when you stop learning*.

## SET YOUR GOALS HIGH

There is nothing wrong with setting your goals extremely high rather than setting mediocre goals where they're easy to reach. I was fortunate that my dad was a high school coach. He ingrained in me at an early age to always set my goals high and to work extremely hard, harder than anyone else thought was reasonable.

Take advantage of your opportunity when it comes. I have been very fortunate that when I have been given an opportunity, I have taken full advantage of it.

You might not be the all-star on the team. You might not be "the" guy that everyone looks at. But if there is a game where there are four or five scouts at your game to watch "the star," and you go out there, and you play hard, play the right way and perform, all of a sudden you catch the eye of a couple scouts and, BOOM!, you've got a college scholarship or maybe a career, professionally.

Take advantage of your opportunities when they arise, work hard, be able to take constructive criticism as a compliment, but at the same time believe in your abilities. If you do that, you'll be amazed at how far you can go. When I was growing up I always loved it when I had somebody that I could ask questions to kind of pick the brain of people where I wanted to be. So don't feel shy to contact me. Feel free to reach out. I love to try and help as many people as I can.

Twitter = @Tooleyj24

E-Mail= Tooleyj24@yahoo.com

# CHAPTER #5 REVIEW

- [ ] College baseball is a different level
- [ ] Professional baseball, will it happen?
- [ ] Draft does not happen
- [ ] Baseball player vs. Position player
- [ ] Plays all nine positions in one game
- [ ] Managing role as a utility player
- [ ] Pre-game routine essential to consistency
- [ ] Playing one pitch at a time
- [ ] Not thinking about routine- just winning this pitch & getting present
- [ ] Learn by watching
- [ ] Inexpensive experience offered
- [ ] Playing past ability level
- [ ] Perfection is unattainable
- [ ] Relaxation is a skill that must be learned
- [ ] Using music as a part of your routine
- [ ] Post-game imagery
- [ ] Control what you can control
- [ ] Batting average is satan
- [ ] If you hit the ball hard, you have good stats
- [ ] You don't have a lot of control in this game
- [ ] We over me mentality
- [ ] Friends and competitors
- [ ] Difference between a friend and teammate
- [ ] Be coachable
- [ ] Baseball is what you do, not who you are

☐ **Mental game shift changes performance**
☐ **Takeaways from Toole**
☐ **Think you can**
☐ **Never listen to the doubters**
☐ **Learn everyday**
☐ **Set your goals high**

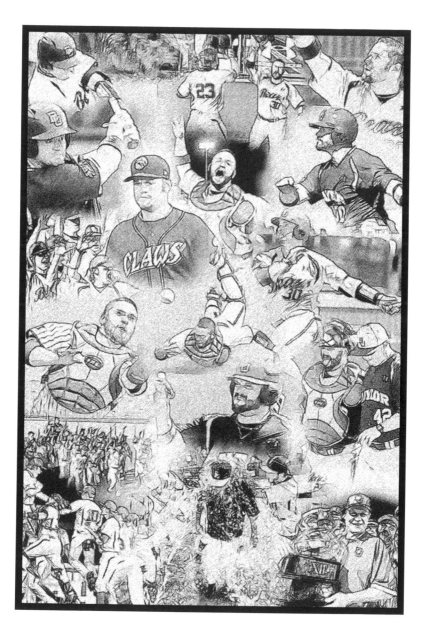

# CHAPTER #6

## JOSH LUDY, FROM BAYLOR BENCH PLAYER
## TO BIG XII PLAYER OF THE YEAR

*J*osh Ludy led the Baylor Bears Baseball program to a *record-setting season in 2012 where the Bears produced the best single season in Big XII baseball history and Ludy took home Big XII Conference Player of the Year and All-American honors. Ludy, now playing in the Philadelphia Phillies farm system, went from bench player to best player with the help of the mental game.*

### FROM FARM LAND TO BIG TIME BASEBALL

I grew up in Portland, Indiana, a small farming town, and played baseball my whole life. When I got into travel baseball they made me a pitcher because I had a strong arm. I played in a select ball tournament at East Cobb in Marietta, Georgia and just happened to have a couple of good games and ended up getting an offer from Baylor. Once I went there, I just fell in love with the place and the people and signed on the spot.

### A CAREER FULL OF EARLY STRUGGLE

When I first got to Baylor, things did not seem to go quite like I had planned for them to. Like many freshmen, I expected to go out there and get a lot of playing time and in my first two seasons I was a bench player. I finally earned a shot my junior year and had an average season.

I started to learn about the mental game from Brian Cain during the fall of my senior year. A lot of what he talked about really clicked for me, especially the breathing and routine.

Being able to slow your heart rate down a little bit and stay in the present moment are two huge aspects of playing baseball consistently. Having a mental and emotional management system to not over-think the game and really just take it one pitch at a time.

## TEAM HAS ONE PITCH WARRIOR ATTITUDE

In 2012, that was our team's mentality, to be a group of one pitch warriors and just play one pitch at a time. We went from being just an average team to having the best season in Big XII history, hosting a regional, super regional and having a great shot at going to Omaha because we were able to stay in the moment and play it one pitch at a time together.

## BREATHING EACH PITCH

I would take a deep breath every pitch when I was hitting. My routine was to step out with one foot and re-do my batting gloves. I would then stare out at the gold ball on top of our flagpole and take a deep breath and get locked back in to playing that next pitch. Once I started taking a breath and using a routine for each pitch, I felt like I was ready to win every pitch when I stepped back into the box.

## FINAL THOUGHTS

My final thought was to simply say "drive it" and have a rhythm with it as I got into the box so that was the only thought in my head at that time. If I started thinking anything other than drive it, I knew I was in a red light and about to give away a pitch or an at-bat. The routine, breath and final thought really helped me to keep it simple, stay in the moment and keep my mind from wondering and play one pitch at a time.

## RECOGNIZE THE RED LIGHT

I was able to recognize red lights when I got that uncomfortable feeling that I was out of my routine and something didn't feel right. That was when I knew that something was a little bit off, and that I was in red lights. That comfort that comes from a routine wasn't there. When I was able to recognize that feeling, I would step out of the batter's box and make sure I really focused on taking that good breath, on my focal point and getting ready before I stepped back into the box.

## RELEASE THE RED LIGHT AND REFOCUS

When I would recognize that red light I would step out with one foot and put the barrel of my bat under my armpit and then undo and re-do my batting gloves once or twice and then get back into my routine of taking a breath on the gold ball on top of the flag pole and get back into the box ready to drive it. For me, the routine really helped to simplify my approach and let me trust the training I had done.

## PLAYING ONE PITCH AT A TIME

Playing one pitch at a time is about staying in the present and staying with that one pitch or that one moment in practice. In baseball, it is so easy to get lost thinking about what might happen down the road or get lost on what just happened.

We were able to stay focused on that pitch and take everything else out of the equation. That approach made the game a lot easier for us and things got a lot simpler. When you play one pitch at a time, success and failure don't matter as much because as soon as that one pitch is over, you are on to the next one and that next pitch is all that matters in that moment and that process just keeps repeating itself. That approach worked really well for us.

## DIFFERENT APPROACH DIFFERENT RESULTS

The approach I took in 2012 was a different approach than I took up to that point in my career. I would think about a lot of things when I was playing before and once I started to work on a routine and playing one pitch at a time, it kind of clicked for me. Once I was able to let go of the past, the future and all the stuff I could not control and just play one pitch at a time, I was able to start clearing things out of my mind and not worry about everything else and it really paid off for me.

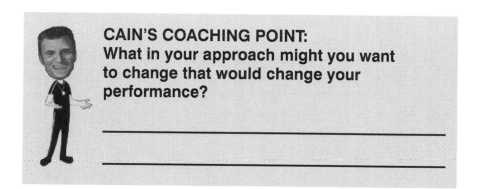

**CAIN'S COACHING POINT:**
**What in your approach might you want to change that would change your performance?**

_____

_____

## DEFENSIVE ROUTINES BEHIND THE PLATE

With catching, it was never that hard for me to stay in the moment mentally, in that ideal mindset where you play your best because there are a lot of things that are going through your head and a lot of things you need to pay attention to. The one thing I changed after learning about the mental game was to take a deep breath and get ready before every pitch to make sure that the pitch that was coming was the only pitch I was focused on at that point in time.

Every catcher is different in their routine. Some catchers get their breath as they get the pitch from the dugout, some take their breath after they get the pitch from the dugout, but before they give the pitcher the sign, and some will take their breath after they give the pitcher the sign. I took my breath after I gave the sign, right before I moved into my stance.

## ADVERSITY MAKES SUCCESS EVEN SWEETER

My suggestion to the player who is not having the success they feel like they should have would be to stay focused on the process and not give up on your goals. There were a couple of times in my career where I thought about transferring from Baylor and finding a new place to go because things were not going the way I thought they would.

Luckily, things didn't work out for me to leave, and I ended up staying at Baylor and things got a heck of a lot better. I ended up having the time of my life staying there and grinding through the adversity. Senior year, I got another opportunity and once you have some success, it makes it even more special if you've gone through a lot of adversity to get to that point.

**CAIN'S COACHING POINT:**
**What is an example of adversity that you have experienced that made your success taste even sweeter?**

_____

_____

## THE PROCESS OVER THE RESULT

Sticking with the process means focusing on what you can control and letting go of what you cannot control. As a hitter, that means letting go of results. If you hit a ball hard and end up getting out, focusing on the process means you celebrate the fact that you hit the ball hard more than you are disappointed that you got out.

Your goal as a hitter is to hit the ball hard because that is what will get you hits over time. In the moment, you may hit a ball hard right at someone and get out, and in the marathon of baseball, hitting the ball hard consistently is what makes you put up the statistics you want at the end of the year.

Focusing on the process means I am not worrying about the result. If I focus on the outcome, I can hit a ball not very well at all and end up getting a hit and if I look at that like I've done something good, it is actually a negative for me long term. Do not fool yourself that getting a hit on a swinging bunt is a quality at-bat. It is far from it. If you think a swinging bunt hit is a quality at-bat, you are not focused on the process and you are counting successes in things you cannot control.

Focusing on the process is about putting good swings on balls and attacking pitches. Win each pitch. That process is more important than the outcome of the at-bat because that process is what will dictate the outcome of that at-bat.

## BEING A GREAT TEAMMATE

In 2012, we had the best season in Baylor and Big XII baseball history. Obviously, we fell one game short of going to Omaha, but that does not take away from the fact that we had a great season. A large part of what made this team so special was everybody was there for each other. Nobody played selfishly.

We all bought into one pitch at a time and if one guy didn't get the job done, another guy was there to pick him up and there was always somebody there. We had each other's back every pitch. Often guys get more concerned with their own stats or the draft and lose focus on the team. For us, it provided a great energy to know that guys were there for us.

Even the guys that didn't play, they were in the dugout and they were locked into team performance and winning pitches, even if they had not played in three weeks. Getting everybody together and all on the same page was an outstanding experience and one I will remember my entire life.

## DUGOUT ENERGY AND INTENT

Until my senior year at Baylor our dugout was pretty quiet. It was a lot like you would see in professional baseball: very matter of fact and low energy. In 2012 we made it a point of emphasis to have a relentless dugout presence and energy and had a system we followed to help keep everybody into the game. Sometimes, we got a little carried away in there, and that is part of college baseball. It made the journey that much more fun.

**CAIN'S COACHING POINT:**
**What is an example of dugout or sideline energy and intent that you and your team could use to help keep you into the game?**

_____

_____

## PROCESS BASED ENERGY SCRIMMAGE

Part of how we developed that new style of play was through something we did in practice all fall. We called it the "Process-Based Energy Scrimmage." We were awarded points for playing the game the right way and for executing the process.

For example, if a pitcher threw strike one or a guy gave a good hard 90 down to first base, that team was awarded with a point on the scoreboard because that was a part of the process that was going to help them win games.

The first time we did it, I wasn't really sure of what was going on. It was pretty fast-paced and chaotic. The goal was to get the game to move fast and to get players to be uncomfortable and it worked. Once we got the hang of it, it was a lot of fun because your focus and awareness was heightened to playing the game the right way. This really helped us learn to stick with the process and not the outcome.

## REGIONAL ADVERSITY, SO WHAT!

At the end of the year, we were the #4 National Seed in the NCAA Tournament and hosted a regional at Baylor. We lost game one to Oral Roberts and when we were in the locker room after the game guys were saying "so what!"

Obviously, we didn't plan on losing game one, and at that point we still would have taken our group of guys head to head with anybody in the country. We had that faith in each other and believed in each other that we were going to get it done. So, while it sucked at the same time, it didn't really bother us either. We welcomed the adversity.

## LOSE GAME TWO OF THE SUPER REGIONAL

We ended up coming back and winning our Regional and then hosted Arkansas for a Super Regional. We won game one and were right there with a chance to win at the end of game two and kind of beat ourselves. The situation was similar to what had happened to us at the end of the 2011 season in a Regional Championship against The University of California, Berkley. But in that moment we had the awareness to know that the game vs. Cal had nothing to do with the game vs. Arkansas and that we still had another chance to come back and play the next day where the year before we did not. We knew we had a one game series left and really approached every game like it was a one game series all year long so it really was not any different for us. We knew all we had to do was play our game one pitch at a time like we had all year.

## BEST TEAM NEVER WINS & THE STREAK

In baseball, the best team never wins. It's always the team that plays the best. In game three, Arkansas just played a little bit better that we did. We played really well all year and set a national record by winning 28 straight games.

We knew about the streak because everybody wanted to talk about it around us, and we would sit around every now and then, just ourselves, and look around at each other and just kind of laugh and say, "What the heck's going on here? What are we doing?"

I remember we went to play Texas A&M at their place on a Friday night and made four errors and still managed to come back and win the game by a run. We were just looking at each other and started laughing. It was a fun ride. A ride that where we enjoyed the journey the whole way. There was never any talk about extending the streak. We only talked about winning pitches, having fun and playing with energy.

## KEEP MOVING FORWARD

I think the best piece of advice I would share with other competitors is to just keep moving forward. Like a UFC fighter, just keep moving forward and stay on the attack. Keep playing one pitch at a time and staying focused on the process. If you do that, you will be surprised at what you can get done. The Baylor team in 2012 did not have many superstars going into the season. We were a bunch of no-name nobodies. Our two starting pitchers threw 85MPH and were 22 and 2 in the Big XII, one of the best baseball conferences in the country. I think those results go to show the power of the mental game and what it can do for you and your team.

# CHAPTER #6 REVIEW

- ☐ From farm land to big time baseball
- ☐ A career full of early struggle
- ☐ Team has one pitch warrior attitude
- ☐ Breathing each pitch
- ☐ Final thoughts
- ☐ Recognize the red light
- ☐ Release the red light and refocus
- ☐ Playing one pitch at a time
- ☐ Different approach – different results
- ☐ Defensive routines behind the plate
- ☐ Adversity makes success even sweeter
- ☐ The process over the result
- ☐ Being a great teammate
- ☐ Dugout energy and intent
- ☐ Process based energy scrimmage
- ☐ Regional adversity, so what!
- ☐ Lose game two of the super regional
- ☐ Best team never wins & the streak
- ☐ Keep moving forward

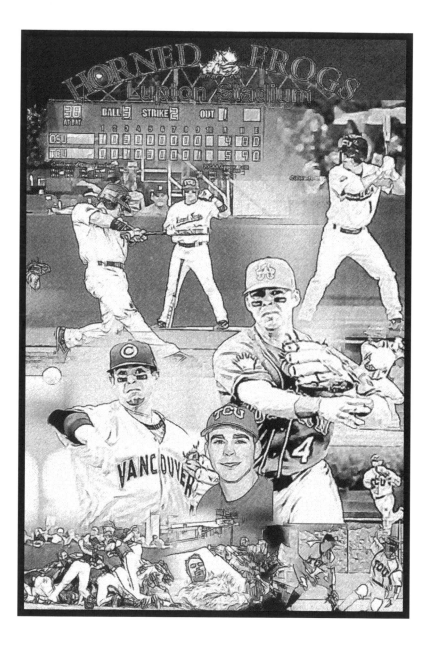

# CHAPTER #7

## BRYAN KERVIN, TCU BASEBALL PLAYER
## USES MENTAL GAME TO SAVE HIS LIFE

*B*ryan Kervin went to Grapevine High School in Grapevine, Texas where he made the varsity baseball team as a freshman and went on to have a fantastic high school baseball career and earned all-state recognition, played on the Texas Sunbelt Team, a team for the top seniors in the state of Texas, and was recruited by some of the top programs in country like TCU, Texas, Arkansas, Nebraska, Clemson and Arizona.

*Kervin went to The University of Arizona out of high school where he started at shortstop for the Wildcats and led them to a Pac-10 championship and was named All-Pac 10 Conference and finished second in freshman of the year voting to current Gold Glove winning shortstop Darwin Barney of the Chicago Cubs and formerly of Oregon State University.*

*After his freshman year at Arizona, Kervin played in the prestigious Cape Cod Summer Baseball League and ran into struggles on the field for the first time in his career, struggling at the plate with a lack of results and statistics that he was not used to.*

*Kervin then transferred to TCU for personal and family reasons and played three seasons for the Horned Frogs at shortstop. He was introduced to the mental game his sophomore year and it really opened his eyes and mind up to a whole different part of the game.*

## INTRODUCTION TO THE MENTAL GAME

I think the mental game is the difference maker at the higher levels of college baseball and will really make or break you. If you truly believe in yourself and believe in your routines and processes for preparing and playing, focusing on the aspects of the game that you can control, then you can achieve anything you set your mind to.

## BE ABLE TO HUMBLE YOURSELF
## SO THE GAME DOES NOT NEED TO

You have to have a foundation and a routine to fall back on every day. If you do not have a routine, you will often let success or failure on a day to day basis have too much impact on how you go about your business. In baseball, when you have success, you can't get too high on yourself or this game will humble you. You need to get back to what you do on a daily basis and trust your preparation and routine. Never get too high on your success or too low on your failure.

**CAIN'S COACHING POINT:**
**In what aspects of your life can you show more humility?**

_____

_____

## TALK THE TALK OR WALK THE WALK

The most successful people I have been around in baseball and in life do not just talk the talk, they walk the walk. After my senior year at TCU, I got drafted by the Toronto Blue Jays and played shortstop in short season A ball and got moved up to play in AA and AAA because someone got hurt. Making the jump from college to AAA in the same season was a challenge, but I was able to hold my own and play with confidence because of my mindset and my approach. I was not going to "step up" because I was in AAA. I was just going to go out there and play my game as it was engrained in me at TCU by our head coach Jim Schlossnagle. Play one pitch at a time, focus on the process and focus on what you want, not what you want to avoid.

That off-season, I was determined to take the next step in my mental game development because I had seen just how important it was to my success in my first season of professional baseball. You could really see the difference between the players that had a mental game background and those that did not in how they handled the success and failure that is part of everyday life in baseball.

I made it a part of my routine to listen to Brian Cain's CDs as I drove to the gym and then started to pass them out to the young kids I would give lessons to and mentor. I felt like I was really coming into my own and getting to know who I was as a person and as a player at that time and felt as if my best baseball was ahead of me.

## RUNNING DOWN A DREAM

My second season of professional baseball in 2009 was my first full season in AA. I was a utility player and was living my dream of playing professional baseball. If you were to ask me in high school if my first full season of professional baseball would be in AA, that would have been a dream come true. However, I was further along than I could've ever expected at that point in my career and it was largely due to the mental game and my ability to go one pitch at a time.

I made it a part of my daily routine to read one of Cain's books or others that were uplifting and helped me to stay on the right course mentally to deal with the grind of the professional season. I always felt that if you are doing the right things and you are working hard, then good things are going to happen.

**CAIN'S COACHING POINT:**
**In order for you to make your dreams a reality, you must first know what your dreams are. What is it that you want to accomplish if you could accomplish anything?**

_____

_____

## MENTAL GAME LUNCHBOX

It's funny, my mom and dad would always put motivational messages in my lunchbox when I was a kid. At the time I thought it was silly, but now realize that by them doing that every day and by me reading those short motivational messages every day, I was building the foundation for my mental game at a very young age.

## HABITS AND PREPARATION ARE ESSENTIAL

I think preparation is just as important, if not more so, than how you perform. You can't just train your physical self. You must also train your mind. I learned that it takes around 21 days of focused and conscious effort to make or break a habit and maybe the most important factor in your success or lack of success are the habits you have.

You truly become the average of the five people who you hang out with most and if you are in an environment around other people who are lifting you up, and they have the same goals, then

124                    www.briancain.com

your behaviors are going to be positive. Unfortunately, it works the same way if you are surrounded by "negaholics" and people who are going to constantly tell you that you can't or that you are not good enough.

We truly have unlimited potential and you are only going to reach your full potential when your conscious thoughts, actions and feelings are positive because you are instilling with all your heart and your mind what it is you want to accomplish vs. what you want to avoid.

It's about applying and preparing yourself with all of your mind and all of your heart and putting yourself in a good environment in order to succeed at whatever you're looking to do. Those conscious thoughts and feelings over the course of time will become your sub-conscious thoughts, which are what guide you to do what you do on a daily basis. Your subconscious mind is like autopilot. When you do something routinely for an extended period of time like driving a car, riding a bike or brushing your teeth, these tasks are taken over by your sub conscious mind and go on autopilot. With hard work and with the right mindset, anything is possible, whether that is as a professional baseball player or for any career out there. The mental game helps you to be at your best when it means the most and it helped me save my life.

## USING THE MENTAL OFF THE FIELD

What I learned from Brian Cain and his teachings truly helped save my life. Controlling what you can control and having a foundation or a focal point that you can look back to when going good and bad help you to be more consistent. The more consistent you can be the more you'll be able to use all of your abilities. I used all of the mental game when I was playing, but really saw the power of living that way when I got sick in November of 2009.

## DIAGNOSED WITH ULCERATIVE COLITIS

I was working hard during the off-season and training seven and eight hours a day through hitting, working out, running and the mental game. I did not always feel great, but was focused on acting differently than how I felt and pushing through. I kept trying to push through and one day almost collapsed at the gym.

I went to the doctor and thought I might have the stomach flu and was diagnosed with ulcerative colitis, which is an autoimmune disease. I found out I was going to be out for a long time. They put me on oral prednisone, which is a steroid that makes you really weak, and it makes you puffy and messes with your hormones. It's not like the anabolic steroids you hear about in sports, it is kind of the opposite. It really wears on your body.

## DISEASE COMES BACK FULL FORCE, 80+ DAYS IN HOSPITAL

I was tapering off the medication in January and looking forward to working out and getting ready to make a comeback when the disease came back. It came back with a vengeance. It came back worse than before.

I went to the hospital January 25 thinking I'd be there a day – maybe three at the most. I ended up spending 41 days straight and over 80 days total in the hospital in 2010. I was told I'd never play baseball again by the doctor. I was told different things that I couldn't control as far as fertility and someday having a family.

At the same time, my girlfriend broke up with me so I was dealing with that emotional stress as well. At that moment, I used the mental game more than I had ever before in my life. My only goal was to live for that present moment, to live that day and to wake up the next day. My faith helped me a lot. I knew not to fear tomorrow because God was with me today.

## TEAM HELPS WITH DAILY GRIND

I was really focused on the people coming in to see me. The support from friends and family from the area coming in to support and encourage me was amazing. I truly fed off of their energy and it made me realize that life is a team sport. Life is truly about being there for each other during any time, especially the difficult ones. I always had support and good teammates throughout the years, but sometimes that goes unnoticed.

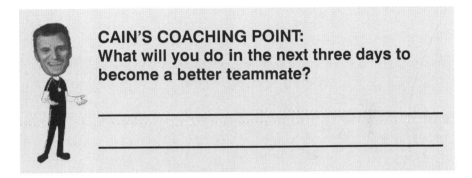

**CAIN'S COACHING POINT:**
**What will you do in the next three days to become a better teammate?**

_____

_____

## BE A GOOD TEAMMATE

I have always been taught by my parents, brothers and sisters to be a good teammate, be a good family member, be a good friend and help encourage someone and lift them up. Good teammates lift each other up.

If I had been acting off of my emotions I would've been a wreck. My emotions in the hospital were not very positive. I was told I could never play baseball again, my girlfriend left me and I was losing weight faster than you can imagine.

While in the hospital, I learned that your heart is in constant communication with your thoughts and your brain. And it's about balancing those two things, thoughts and emotions. You really have to act differently and think differently than how you feel.

I just really learned the importance of support, encouragement, love and belief and the importance of having each other's back. In this game of life we are all in a "universe." "Uni-" (meaning one) and then "verse" (as in a song). Universe loosely means "one song."

If you are in a band or an orchestra, everybody has to play their own part. In baseball, we all have to play our own part. It is the coming together as one while still playing your own part that makes this game so special. In baseball or in life, nobody can be a one man band. We all need each other.

 **www.BrianCain.com/experience for a list of what Bryan Kervin and Brian Cain think are the characteristics of top teammates on and off the field.**

## STUDY OF WATER AND ENERGY

I saw that someone did a study with two cups of water where they had one that was in a room where positive words were spoken and positive music was played and one in a different room where negative music was played and negative words were spoken. Over the course of time, the molecules that made up the water were charged significantly differently based on the environment that they were in. I know it sounds weird, but when you think about it, our bodies are made up of 70% water. So what we put into our mind, negative or positive, will over the course of time change who you are.

## CONTROL WHAT YOU CAN CONTROL

"Control what you can control" really is the foundation of the mental game for me. We cannot control many of the things that happen to us, we cannot control certain situations, but we can control our perspective and how we look at and respond to certain situations.

**CAIN'S COACHING POINT:**
**What are the factors in your life and your performance that you can control that you need to lock in on over the next three days?**

_____

_____

## NO TIME FOR FEELING SORRY FOR YOURSELF

If I start feeling sorry for myself because I'm in the hospital, this world's not going to stop for me. If you're going to start looking down instead of looking up, you're going to get run over and trampled. But if you look up and look from a different perspective and look at your challenges and say, "This is only making me stronger. This is only going to make me be better because of this experience." You are going to increase your chances of coming out on the positive end of things.

I learned to rely and lean on my faith, my family and my friends during these difficult times and really focus on what I can control. I truly believe that focusing on what I can control: my effort, my attitude and my perspective, game me the strength I needed and provided the perseverance that saved my life.

## CODE RED RESPONSE TEAM – NEAR DEATH

I had surgery on Monday, February 8, 2010. That Saturday, February 6, 2010 the doctors had to call a response team to my room and a code red over the hospital as my heart rate shot up to 190. My temperature shot up to 105, and I was throwing up gallons and gallons of blood. This was after I had my colon taken out. They called in my family because they were not sure I was going to make it.

## EXTREME PAIN AND PEACE

I was in extreme pain but was at peace because I truly believed, with all my heart, that I had done the things I needed to do. No matter what happened that day, I knew it was in God's hands. And I knew that my family was there and knew everything was going to be OK.

It is funny to say, but the person that was hurting the least during the toughest time of my life was me, the one who was going through it. It wasn't because I'm a strong person or I'm tough or anything like that. It's because of the people around me: my family, my friends and the TCU coaches and my teammates who gave me the core beliefs and values that helped me persevere.

## THE ESSENTIAL BELIEFS

If I had to go through and list what my core beliefs are, I would start by saying that the foundation to strength and perseverance is controlling what you can control.

Faith is critical. I was in God's word and everybody was praying for me. Faith is something that just totally impacted my life and helped heal me.

Passion: I was so passionate about each and every moment that I was putting all of my heart and all my energy into, at that time, just getting past the next minute. It wasn't about what's going to happen tomorrow or if I was ever going to get to eat at Chick-fil-A again. I couldn't even lift my legs six inches off the bed.

I was passionate about doing my rehab with all of my heart and all my energy, that even though my energy levels were not there, I found it deep within to be passionate for my family and for the people that were up there, for the people that were hurting worse than I was because I knew everything was going to be OK. And everything was in control because I had prepared myself before that.

Have faith, passion and purpose. I started to do everything with a purpose for every breath at that time. I started to look at my family different, being thankful and realizing the purpose we're here in this world is because we're here to make a difference in others' lives. It's just a different perspective that I have had on life since that whole experience.

Having a positive attitude is also essential. There was not one time I let myself think a negative thought or worry or doubt when I was in the hospital. I think that for a person who strives to be positive no matter what, positive is only like a freight train on a track of rusted rails. If you don't have the core beliefs, faith, passion, purpose and a plan, then that positive thinking is only good for so long.

I had to have a plan to just pick my legs up, a rehab plan, to sit up in my bed before I would be able to walk. A plan to go home, to walk down my hall and back, to walk to my mailbox and back, to my neighbor's mailbox and back. I had to have a plan for the process of healing and for the process of recovery. I couldn't just expect to snap my fingers and be healthy again. For me, it was about preparation, having a strategy, having a vision and having small goals and long-term goals, but always getting back to the present, being able to compensate and adjust if things did not go as planned and then get back to playing the next pitch, which for me was at times, getting another breath in and to stay alive for one more minute.

## FOCUS ON THE NEXT PITCH IN YOUR LIFE

Focusing on that next pitch in life is critical. If you made an error, it's not about that error anymore, it is in the past. Think about that next pitch and making that next play. Regardless of the past, you have to believe in yourself, believe that you're going to make the game-winning play when the game's on the line. No one will even remember that error you made if you make that game winning play.

I had to live in the present moment of each second, millisecond, in order to save my life. I had to concentrate on how I was going to get through this for my family, for the ones who have been there for me and have supported me the whole time – my friends, everybody around me, the community, everybody that has thrown me a prayer. I'm going to show them I'm going to rise up, and I'm going to conquer this disease. And I'm going to show them that nothing is impossible in life.

The only thing that holds you back is you. The only limitation you have on yourself is you. That's why I motivate myself daily. We are humans and we all make mistakes. That's just how we are, nobody is perfect. It is all about how you respond to adversity and your respond-ability.

The enemy wants to create separation between relationships, whether that's separation between you and God, separation between you and others or separation between you and yourself. And when that happens, you start to lose trust in each other and trust in yourself.

You start not believing that you are going to win. Pride prevents and humility heals. So make sure that you are humble and realize that it is not about you, but it is about others.

Until I went through what I went through in the hospital, I believed in all the outside things that I had done for my preparation but did not truly believe in myself. I really believed, in that moment, that no matter what happened that day, I was going to survive that day because of the people around me and the things I've learned and controlling what I could control in that present moment and focusing on living that present moment with a purpose and with a passion.

## I DON'T FEEL SORRY FOR ME, WHY DO YOU?

People would look at me and feel sorry for me. When people told me they felt sorry for me, I said, "I feel sorry for you".

If you haven't had a life-changing experience, you may not know of the peace that I am talking about. It was an indescribable peace and a change that has only been for the better. Life is all about perspective, attitude and how you take things.

Good teams have the perspective of, no matter what happens throughout the season, throughout the grind, that they are going to win the next pitch. They're not worried about the game before or the game after. They are totally locked into the present and on winning this particular pitch. They believe that they're going to overcome whatever adversity comes their way during the season.

**CAIN'S COACHING POINT:**
What are some areas in your life that you have felt sorry for yourself for having to deal with? Write these areas below and let this exercise be the STOP of you feeling sorry for yourself because these challenges have made you stronger and the champion that you are today!

_____

_____

## ATTITUDE OF GRATITUDE

I also learned to have an attitude of gratitude, grateful for everyday. Don't just be grateful for the big obvious things like family, friends and the ability to play baseball. Be grateful for the little things that most people don't even think about from day-to-day until you're on your death bed and not sure if you are going to make it or not.

When that day comes, you will ask yourself, "Did I do what I needed to do in this world to leave a legacy? Did I do everything I could or did I just kind of get by? Did I get a little bit out of my talent or did I get everything out of my talent?"

Be grateful for the little things in life because they can get taken away from you faster than you expect.

When I was sitting in that hospital bed, and was in the hospital over 80 days, there were times when I didn't eat for four weeks. I went from 190 to 120 pounds. There were times when I would just have done anything for a drop of water. I had thrush in my throat where it's strep throat times 100. I wasn't even able to drink water. I learned to be grateful for the little things in this country and to appreciate the little things that we're blessed with.

### *If you're not grateful for a little then how are you going to be grateful for a lot?*

You also have to be fearless. "Fear not tomorrow for God is here today." It is not about what game is tomorrow, what you are going to do tomorrow, what big college party you are going to go to tomorrow night. It's about not looking forward, fearing tomorrow or worrying about what things tomorrow may bring.

Success is about living fearlessly in the present moment, it's about playing the game, playing the right way and not letting yourself get away from being passionate and playing with all of your heart, all your energy and controlling what you can control.

## SPRING TRAINING AGAIN... FINALLY

The doctor said that I wouldn't have made it if I wasn't in the shape I was in or the age I was at. Things happened for me that

2012 off season in a totally different way than I could have ever expected. I was working hard and dedicated myself to the sport I love. I was able to recover and get back to spring training in 2011 and I went in with an attitude of gratitude. I was no longer concerned about making it to the big leagues or at what level I would break spring training, I was just taking it all in and truly enjoying the opportunity to play like I never had before.

As I got through extended spring training and was getting back into playing shape, I was sent to short season A in Vancouver. I focused on making a difference there and sharing what I had learned with my teammates. I tried to share with them what I had learned about the mental game of baseball and the mental game of life because if these skills can save my life, they sure can help you to play better baseball and have better relationships with your family, friends, teammates and self.

## PREPARATION IS THE KEY TO SUCCESS

I think the physical and mental preparation that you put in are the biggest factors in your performance. In baseball and in life, you are going to get out what you put in. Mental imagery and visualizing, putting your mind into those conscious thoughts and feelings so it becomes sub-conscious when you step in the batter's box, focusing on your breathing and slowing the game down are all parts of the preparation process.

You can't just do your breathing exercises and work on routines two days before the season starts, you must work to instill those conscious thoughts and feelings so it becomes a habit, and part of who you are and what you do on a daily basis. Success is really a lifestyle, not an event.

You shouldn't just take pride in your schoolwork. You must be a good teammate, be a good family member and do something to help someone else out. Go out of your way to put the focus on others and to spread the wealth of the gifts you have been given.

Get the focus off of you and onto helping others, and you'll find that instead of trying to find a temporary happiness or a positive feeling in that moment, you'll find a joy that lasts forever. It's a peace that you feel and that fosters inside of you when you work to make others better.

Follow Bryan on Twitter @bckervin

# CHAPTER #7 REVIEW

- [ ] Introduction to the mental game
- [ ] Be able to humble yourself so the game does not need to
- [ ] Talk the talk or walk the walk
- [ ] Running down a dream
- [ ] Mental game lunchbox
- [ ] Habits and preparation are essential
- [ ] Using the mental game off the field
- [ ] Diagnosed with ulcerative colitis
- [ ] Disease comes back full force – 80+ days in hospital
- [ ] Team helps with daily grind
- [ ] Be a good teammate
- [ ] Study of water and energy
- [ ] Control what you can control
- [ ] No time for feeling sorry for yourself
- [ ] Code Red response team – near death
- [ ] Extreme pain and peace
- [ ] The essential beliefs
- [ ] Focus on the next pitch in your life
- [ ] I don't feel sorry for me, why do you?
- [ ] Attitude of gratitude
- [ ] Spring training again... finally
- [ ] Preparation is the key to success

# CHAPTER #8

## RYAN CAMERON, NO PLACE IN BASEBALL FOR THE PASSIVE PITCHER

*R*yan Cameron grew up in the small town of Williamstown, Massachusetts and went on to be an All-Atlantic 10 Pitcher for the University of Massachusetts and an 11th round pick of the Colorado Rockies in 1998.

*Cameron experienced success at all levels of Minor League Baseball, spending five seasons with the Rockies, two seasons with the Red Sox, a spring training with the Marlins and three seasons with the Phillies. Cameron also played internationally in Puerto Rico and Venezuela. Now a private pitching instructor in the northeast, Cameron shares his expensive experience through more than ten years in minor league baseball.*

### WHAT IS THE MENTAL GAME

There are two aspects of The Mental Game of baseball. 1.) The psychological aspects of performance in the mental game are about developing the skill set to deal with the adversity that is at the core of the game and 2.) The strategic and mental aspects to help you understand the ins and outs of how to play the game.

A lot of people think the mental game is just a concept or an idea but it's much more than that. It is a lifestyle that helps you to get the most out of your ability both on and off the diamond and helps you when you are out on the mound to better understand the game situation, the inning, count, score and what you are trying to do with the pitch you are about to throw.

## ADVERSITY IS ESSENTIAL

Adversity is a huge part of baseball and knowing how to handle the frustration and failure that is part of the game is key to your success. You have to accept that mistakes are going to happen and be able to put them behind you and get to the next pitch before that failure snowballs on you.

You are going to deal with adversity, the politics of the game, and situations during every pitch in the game. The other team is going to try to speed the game up on you and you have to keep the game at your pace to have success when it means the most.

**CAIN'S COACHING POINT:**
**What are some adverse situations that have happened in your career that you let become bigger than they needed to be?**

_____

_____

## TWO PACES TO THE GAME

There are two paces to baseball: the external pace that you do not control and the internal pace that you do control. The external pace has to do with the crowd, field conditions, umpires, other team, coaches and your teammates while the internal pace is how you are in control of yourself. The mental game is about having control over yourself, your thoughts, actions and personal performance.

## KNOW GAME SITUATION,
## EACH PITCH HAS A PURPOSE

You want to constantly know the game situation and know what you are trying to do with each pitch. If it is the first inning and I run the count to 2-0 on the second batter of the game with nobody on and one out, I am going to throw a fastball. It's my best pitch. Here you go, try and hit it. If you hit a home run, it is 1-0 in the first inning. No big deal. Tip your cap to the hitter.

I am going to try to locate that pitch in or out. I am certainly not going to give you a cookie. The inning, count, score and situation dictate that I am going to throw a fastball in that situation.

I am not going to walk you. I am not going to give you an opportunity to get a runner on and hit a two-run homer. I'm going to go right after you, play the odds, play the percentages, and locate a fastball.

In the eighth inning and a 1-0 or 2-0 ballgame, if I go 2-0, what's my best pitch that day? I always think inning, count, situation and score. Where are we at right now? It helps me to stay in the present moment and formulate the best possible plan for that pitch. If we are in the eighth inning and it is 2-0, what has worked for me today? If it has been my change-up, guess what? 2-0 count, you are getting my changeup. If my best pitch has been my breaking ball, that is what you will get. If my best pitch that day has been my fastball, that is what you will get. Never make a mistake with your third-best pitch. Never make a mistake with your second-best pitch. Be ultra aggressive and attack with whatever's working for you that day.

**CAIN'S COACHING POINT:**
**What does being ultra aggressive and under control look like in your performance?**

_____

_____

## AWARENESS OF WHAT IS WORKING

Everyone knows that Roger Clemens has an outstanding fastball. That's his best pitch. But, today, it might not be his best pitch. Today his split-finger or his slider or his cutter might be his best pitch. Being aware of what your strengths are and how they change day to day is key for consistent peak performance. The game of baseball is a chameleon. It changes from day to day. It changes from pitch to pitch. And you have to have awareness if you are going to be a consistent performer. You have got to recognize where you are in that present moment and make those slight adjustments and execute.

## CHECK POINTS

I use the inning, count, situation and score as a mnemonic and a way to bring me back to reality. There are checkpoints for me in each situation just like I use a focal point on the rubber and a breath as part of my routine check points. Those check points keep you in the game because if you go out there and you just think, "Hey, my strength is my fastball" and you are in the eighth inning, 2-0, and you throw a fastball to a fastball hitter, it is going to get crushed. You're going to look back at the tape, and you're going to say, "Man, my curveball was so good that day. I should've thrown a curve ball." Having a routine and check points both mentally and strategically helps you to stay in the present and gives you the best chance for success on a consistent basis.

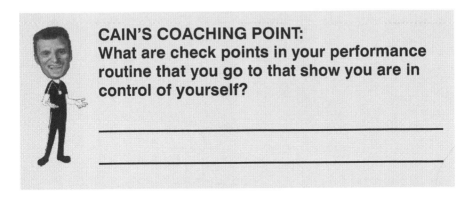

**CAIN'S COACHING POINT:**
**What are check points in your performance routine that you go to that show you are in control of yourself?**

_____

_____

## AWARENESS AND CONTROL

The mental game is all about awareness because what you are aware of you can control and what you are unaware of will control you. If you are not aware of what your best pitch is in that outing you will make mistakes in critical situations. You have got to be aware of each pitch and that is how you play: one pitch at a time. It comes down to playing at your pace.

## THE SPEED OF BASEBALL

Baseball can speed up on you in a hurry. When you let what is going on around you dictate how you go about executing a pitch or a delivery, fielding a baseball etc., your chances of making a mistake improve dramatically.

Take a common situation: runners at first and second, nobody out and you know they are bunting. Everybody in the ball park knows they're going to lay down a bunt. A guy lays down a picture-perfect bunt to third base. You have all day to throw this baseball, and what do you do? You don't set your feet.

You open up, and you throw it down the right-field line. Two runs score and you have a runner on second base with nobody out. However, if you take your time, do it like you have done it a thousand times in practice, recognize the situation and adjust to the play, you have one out and runners on second and third.

You have a lot of options as a pitcher in that situation. You can walk the next guy and set up a double-play, be ultra aggressive and challenge a guy inside and take the safe risk that you may hit him in that situation, etc.

I am going to pick a former teammate of mine, Juan Pierre, as an example. The guy is a base stealer. He is a guy who can lay down a drag-bunt and make things happen with his speed.

If you look at him and say, "Oh man, this guy's fast. I've got to be faster," you beat yourself. You've got to look at it like, "This guy's fast. He's going to play at my pace. I'm going to slow him down. I'm going to hold the ball. I'm going to throw over. I'm going to step off. I control the pace of this game."

As the pitcher, you have the ball. You control the pace of the game. As soon as you understand that, as soon as you believe in that, you'll shut down the running game and you'll be ten steps ahead of everybody else.

If I was a hitter, I would think I had control of the pace of the game because nothing can happen until I step in the batter's box. The fight for control is really a battle of wills and making sure that you play at your pace. What it comes down to is the person who's more mentally conditioned is the one who controls the pace of the game. Although the pitcher does dictate when they throw the pitch, the hitter still dictates when they get in the batter's box and they're ready to see that pitch.

If I am speaking to pitchers, I say when the hitter's not in the batter's box, there's no game. The game starts when the hitter gets to the batter's box, so as a hitter *you* are not really controlling anything. It is a game of cat and mouse that we all play, fighting for control. The key is that you have control of yourself in any and all situations.

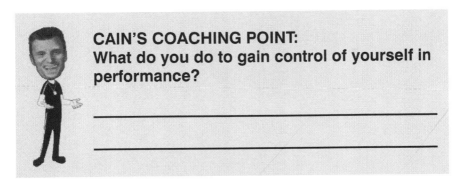

**CAIN'S COACHING POINT:**
**What do you do to gain control of yourself in performance?**

_____

_____

## PRACTICE CONTROLLING THE PACE

You have to practice controlling the pace of the game. Holding the baseball as a pitcher sounds like the easiest thing in the world, but it is not. Holding the baseball on the mound in front of 15,000 people is one of the toughest things you will ever do.

You might balk. The runner may run, the hitter might bunt, fans are going to be yelling your name. If you are on the road or at home, people in the stands will yell at you for holding the ball because they don't understand the game. You have to let go of all those things. They are out of your control. You control the game. Not one of those people are going to do anything to affect your performance unless you let them. That runner isn't going to do anything that is going to affect your performance, unless you let him. You are in control.

A large part of staying in control of yourself is about the deep breath. If you see the pitcher take the deep breath then get on the mound, you know he is doing something to stay in control of himself. When you see the hitter step out of the box, look at their bat and take a deep breath, you know that hitter is getting into the box on his pace and his plan. The pitcher may hold the ball, but the hitter can always step out of the box. If you do not feel like you are ready, either step out of the box or off the rubber.

**CAIN'S COACHING POINT:**
**What type of pace do you play at? When have you experienced the pace of the game speeding up or slowing down?**

_____

_____

## HORROR MOVIES TELL ALL

How many times have you seen a horror movie when the victim can take a deep breath? Never. Why? They are scared, in red lights and are too caught up in the moment. They need to take a deep breath, gain control and get back to the present. They need to focus on "what is" and not "what if." "What is" brings you to the present, "what if" puts you in the past or the future.

## WHAT TO DO WITH THE SCARED PLAYER

If you are a coach and have a player who you think is scared, you must reinforce confidence. You have to remind them of why they are good and help to build their confidence. I played with guys who threw 95 miles an hour and were scared to death to throw a fastball. You have to trust yourself, whether you throw 70 miles an hour or you throw 100. You have to trust your stuff. You have to realize that the odds are always in your favor as a pitcher. The best hitter is going to get out seven out of ten times. The odds are ALWAYS in your favor. If you had a seven out of ten chance to win one million dollars but to get those odds you had to put a one thousand dollar bet on the table right now, you would do it in a second.

So why wouldn't you throw your best pitch with conviction when you need it the most? You have a seven-out-of-ten chance that the hitter will get himself out. He might get a hit. He might hit a home run that the guys talk about for the next 20 years. It's one pitch. Whether it has a good result or a bad result, learn from it and move on to the next one. Do not concern yourself with failure. Failure is positive feedback and is one of the best things that can happen to you as a pitcher because failure will make you better. Failure is a necessary stop on the road to success. If you go out and throw a no-hitter, you don't get anything out of it except for a few interviews, a few pictures, a few memories and a few souvenirs. Once you step on the mound again, it makes no difference what you did the last time out, good and bad.

## EVALUATE GOOD AND BAD, BE AGGRESSIVE

You have to always evaluate what did you do well and what you can improve on. What did you execute well and not so well? Success on the mound always comes back to execution. It comes back to aggressiveness and intent. In my opinion, as a pitcher, if you're aggressive and you go out there with a purpose and intent for each pitch, you are going to give yourself the best chance for positive results.

If you are tentative and meek and you are just there to throw strikes, you could execute every single pitch and get hammered because you are throwing strikes right down the middle of the plate. There is NOWHERE in baseball or in life that you will be successful by being passive; you must be aggressive and have intent in all you do. If you are not going to pitch aggressively and challenge the hitter to beat you with your best pitch, you might as well not even be out there.

## THROWING STRIKES IS NOT ENOUGH

Hitters get themselves out. As a pitcher, the goal is not to throw strikes because if you have an 0-2 count on a guy and you want to throw the ball in the dirt or you want to throw that pitch six inches outside, you are not trying to throw a strike. Your only goal on the mound is to execute quality pitches with aggression and intent.

All you're trying to do is make pitches. As a pitcher, your job is to be a professional target-hitter, a professional glove pounder. My job is to pound the mitt and pound the mitt with conviction. If I am throwing a fastball outside, I am committing to that pitch, and I am getting after that fastball outside. I am hitting the mitt or my spot.

I am not trying to get guys out because I cannot control getting outs. I am not trying to throw strikes because I am not trying to throw strikes with every pitch. I am trying to execute one pitch at a time, with aggressiveness and intent. I am trying to pound the mitt. And if I pound the mitt, I'm giving myself the best chance to be successful.

**CAIN'S COACHING POINT:**
If you are a pitcher, what is your goal? Remember, your goal must be in your control. If you are not a pitcher, what is your goal?

_____

_____

## PUT YOURSELF IN THE SCARY SITUATION

Barry Bonds just stepped up to plate, and you have to get him out. What are you going to do? Take a second, think about that. What are you going to throw to Barry Bonds? You are scared to death right now. What are you thinking?

"Oh my God, he hit 73 home runs. He's the best home-run hitter of all time. He's Barry Bonds."

Now you are starting to think outside of your ability and outside of your control because you do not control getting him out. When you focus on aspects of performance or goals outside of your control, you increase your stress and you are more likely to not be aggressive.

I don't care if it's Barry Bonds or Brian Cain, there should be no difference in your mental approach. Barry Bonds gets out, too. He hasn't hit .400. He's never hit .400, *only* .370 once in his career in 2002 and he is a career .298 hitter. He's going to hit some home runs. You tip your hat when he hits it. He's a great Major Leaguer. Being aggressive is the key. As a pitcher, you can't get hitters out, and the goal is not even to throw strikes. The goal is pound the mitt with conviction.

## HUMBLE CONFIDENCE

The best pitchers I have been around have all had a humble confidence. They had the confidence that they could get anyone out in any situation by making pitches. They were also humble in that they knew they could get hit by anyone in any situation. Humble confidence keeps you honest and hungry in your pursuit of excellence.

In any situation, I always come back to inning, count, situation, score. With an 0-2 count, you may or may not want to throw a strike. It depends on the situation. If you are facing a guy who's hitting .130, you are absolutely going to throw a strike. Why not?

He's hitting .130. That means barely one time out of every ten he's getting a hit. Go right after him. If you are facing a guy hitting .330, 0-2 count, what is your best pitch that day?

## BALANCE, EXTENSION, AGGRESSIVE EXECUTION

When it comes to pitching, I focus on three things.

    1. Dynamic balance

    2. Extension

    3. Aggressive execution of the pitch.

I think you have to have dynamic balance at the beginning of your delivery, at the top of your delivery, and throughout your delivery. At the end of your delivery you have to have extension towards your target. If you don't have extension, you cut the ball off and will have no idea what it's going to do. If you have accomplished dynamic balance and extension, you have physically given yourself the best chance to execute a pitch and throw it where you intended to throw it. When you throw the ball where you want to throw it, you give yourself the best chance for a successful outcome and are already a success within the process of controlling what you can control.

## THE LAW OF AVERAGE

Skip Bertman, former baseball coach at LSU, talked about the law of average. The law of average says that when you play the game of baseball four things can happen.

    1. You can play well and win.

    2. You can play well and lose.

    3. You can play lousy and win.

    4. You can play lousy and lose.

150          

The law of average says that the team that plays well is the team that's giving themselves the best chance to win. There are no guarantees that if you play well you're going to win because you may have brought up an opponent that's more talented than you or an opponent that plays well or an opponent that plays a little better than you, even though you did play well. It is the same with pitching. If you throw that pitch with conviction and you throw it to the spot you intended to throw it to, that makes you successful regardless of the result. It is your quality pitch percentage that will determine your long term success.

**CAIN'S COACHING POINT:**
**As you look back at your career, how has the law of average shown up in your performance?**

_____

_____

## LEARN FROM EVERYONE

I try to take something from everybody I talk to, play for and play with. I was fortunate in that I got to meet some pretty good baseball players and my openness to asking questions and being a leader allowed me to take something from everyone.

## GREG MADDUX GOT IT

I saw an interview once where Greg Maddux said he would evaluate himself after each performance, good and bad, always knowing that his pursuit was to get better and be the best he could be. He would also spend time looking for the positives when he had a poor performance. He talked about how that would help him to create an even keel and deal with the peaks and valleys that you pitch in. Eliminating the snowball effect of one poor performance leaking into another is key. You have to separate yourself from your performance and go out there and give it all you have that day, learn from it and then leave it behind, both good and bad.

You can have a great year with bad outings. In 2006, I pitched in Scranton, AAA with the Phillies, had around a three earned run average, but in one game I had an inning where I gave up five runs on eight hits in two-thirds of an inning. I could have let that one poor outing ruin my entire year. I could have looked at that like, "Man, I don't have the stuff to get people out at AAA. I'm done. I need to retire." I chalk it up to just being a bad day. Everyone has them.

I went back to the clubhouse and as hard as it was, I asked myself, what did I do well? When I struck a guy out, I threw a great curve ball. I threw a couple of good changeups, and I took that positive out of the worst outing of my career. With a strong perspective, my next outing was a positive outing where I pitched two scoreless.

## PERFECTION IS SATAN

A lot of baseball players are perfectionists. If they throw a one-hitter, they are pissed because they didn't throw the no-hitter. It is crazy.

The best guys take the positive from the negative performance and really break down and evaluate their great performances and take out the things they can do to get better.

I remember, watching Maddux when I was a high school pitcher, and he'd strike a guy out, and you'd see him curse himself out on the mound. When I was young, I thought that was what great pitchers did. I would strike some one out in high school and I'd be cursing myself out on the mound. I did not understand why Maddux was doing what he was doing. And as I got older and got around better coaches and understood the game more, I learned that Maddux had a great focus on the process and evaluated his success on where he threw the ball. If he struck out a guy with a mistake, he was more upset with himself than he was if he gave up a hit on a quality pitch. He understood the process of pitching and controlling what you can control. He focused on what he can control in making pitches and took the result out of it because he could not control the result.

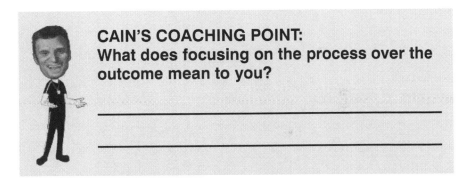

**CAIN'S COACHING POINT:**
**What does focusing on the process over the outcome mean to you?**

_____

_____

## YOU CAN NOT MAKE UP FOR THE PAST

Another mistake I see pitchers make is that they try to make up for the mistakes in the past. If they had that one bad outing they go out the next time trying to make up for it thinking that they have to do better than the last time instead of focusing on what they are doing in the current time. They are essentially pitching with one foot stuck in the past. When Babe Ruth would strike out and reporters would ask him after the game what he thought about after striking out, he said he would think about hitting homeruns. Babe Ruth didn't focus on the negative parts of the game, he focused on the positive and what he was trying to do.

## BE A STUDENT OF THE GAME

Bob McClure pitched for 22 years in the Major Leagues and was a very good left handed pitcher. Mac was one of the first coaches I played for who invested the time to figure me out. I don't think there are any cookie cutter approaches that work in baseball. Mac did not try to change how I threw the ball, he just wanted me to have the three absolutes to pitching: dynamic balance, extension and aggressive execution of the pitch.

He did not care how we did it. He said you can stand on your head and if you achieve a dynamic balance, extension and aggressive execution of the pitch then stand on your head.

A lot of pitching coaches really don't take that approach. They try to clone you mechanically and it takes the athleticism right out of you. They believe you have to be in the Double L Position, you can't throw across your body or have an unorthodox delivery. Mac was the one guy I played for who embraced it and opened my eyes to the fact that there are a lot of different ways to throw the baseball.

I have always been a student of the game because I have always held a very high respect for the guys who have done it. I think, today, you go through the game and you meet so many players who do not have a respect for the history of the game and focus too much on what they can get from the game vs. what they can give back to the game.

At the end of the day, the game is so much bigger than we are as individuals. As players, we are very disposable. You could take everybody in the Major Leagues right now and throw them out the window, and you'd have a whole new Major Leagues tomorrow. The game goes on and it owes you nothing.

Understand where the game has come from, understand where some of these great players are and what they've done. The guys who have done it, those are the guys who you want to spend time with and learn from. These are the guys you want to watch a DVD about, meet in person, and talk pitching or hitting with. I am always cautious of the guru who has never been to the top of the mountain and tells you the best way to get there.

**CAIN'S COACHING POINT:**
**What are ways that you can demonstrate being a student of the game? Who is one of the best students of the game that you know? What is it about that person that makes you say that?**

_____

_____

## TAKE ADVANTAGE OF OPPORTUNITIES

Take advantage of any chance you get to talk to an old-timer who has been around the game. Get their inexpensive experience. Ask them what they know now that they wish they knew when they were just getting started. Part of what made Mac so great was all of his stories. Any time I got to sit and talk with him in the years I had him as a coach, he told stories about guys and how they did it and they were all different.

He talked a lot about their different approaches and through that sharing of their experiences I was better able to formulate my own approach using the inexpensive experience.

## DIFFERENT APPROACH FROM AMATEUR TO PRO

The game itself is the same at the amateur level and professional level. It really does not change all that much. But the approach in college to pro is vastly different.

In college and high school there is a heightened sense of urgency because you have to get it done today because you only play three or four games a week and in high school you play 20 games a season, in college only 56. At the amateur level there is a greater sense of urgency to get it done, whereas at the professional level you play 160 games a year and if you lost today, so what, you have tomorrow.

Mac really made me understand that when you go from the amateur to the professional game, that sense of urgency can kill you because they play 160 games.

## TEWKS SHARES HIS EXPERIENCE

Bob Tewksbury was our sport psychologist with the Boston Red Sox and he was unbelievable. "Tewks" is a student of the game, played in the Major Leagues, was an all-star and actually went back to school and got a degree in sports psychology at Boston University.

When I met him I was with the Boston Red Sox, and the politics of the game kind of got under my skin. I started letting things outside of my control, control my approach, control my desire, control my love for the game. I spent a pretty good deal of that season as a miserable man, bitter at the game and I didn't play well because of it.

Tewks pulled me aside one day and said, "What are you doing? When you're out on that mound, man, it's all about you. You know, it's not about the game. It's about you. Who cares about anything else? You can't control whether your Minor League director sends you down. You can't control whether your high school coach benches you. You can't control whether your college coach doesn't want you to throw in the big game. These are things out of your control. You can't control whether a guy hits a great 0-2 curve ball down at his ankles out of the ball park. You are beating yourself."

And as soon as I started to listen to what he was saying, understand what he was saying and apply it to my performance, I really started to love the game again and play better because my focus was solely on what I could control. From that moment forward I had more success in my career than I had ever had before. He reinforced the importance of controlling what you can control and going out there to be aggressive. Play as hard as you can. Play as well as you can. And when things don't go your way, learn from it and flush it.

As a pitcher, once that ball leaves your hand, it's all out of your control. Physically and mentally give yourself the best chance for success by controlling what you can control physically and mentally with that ball in your hand. If you do everything within your realm of control to give yourself the best chance to be successful, the law of average is going to give you a greater chance to win.

## MEETING THE MASTER OF THE MENTAL GAME

In 2002, I got to go to Cal State Fullerton and visit a friend of mine, Ken Ravizza, who was teaching sport psychology in graduate school. I got to spend some time with Ken, who wrote *Heads Up Baseball,* go to some of his classes and kind of get a classroom feel for the mental game. That was the first time I was ever really introduced to it on a personal level. This was before I had met Tewks with the Red Sox.

When I met Ken, he said something to me in the first hour I met him that has stuck with me to this day. He talked about playing one pitch at a time and once he said that, pitching became a lot easier mentally because all I had to do was have a plan for one pitch. I did not have to focus on the entire sequence I was going to throw, just that one pitch.

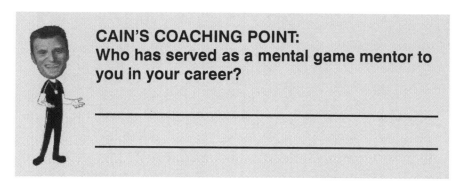

**CAIN'S COACHING POINT:**
**Who has served as a mental game mentor to you in your career?**

_____

_____

## ONE PITCH AT A TIME

That approach of going one pitch at a time helped me to make the game easier from a mental standpoint. The game is never easy, but I had a much simpler plan. There were times I used to go out and I used to think, "I got to strike this guy out," and I would be thinking about the third pitch instead of the one I was about to throw. Or I would think, "I've got to get this guy to hit my curve ball after this fastball," and I would start thinking too many pitches ahead and beat myself.

Coaches always say that you need to have a plan, but a plan doesn't mean go out and know what five pitches you are going to throw to this hitter in this at-bat? The plan is, "I'm going to execute this pitch. I'm going to pound these guys in or I am going to pitch backwards," but it must be one pitch at a time.

Whatever your pitch selection, it has to be one pitch at a time. If I go out and I pitch one pitch at a time mentally it means I am totally into the present moment and focused on that pitch. I may have an idea of what sequence I am going to throw that hitter, but that sequential thinking happens with my feet off the rubber.

When my feet get on the rubber it is one pitch at a time.

I take information from that last pitch and use it to formulate my plan for the next one. If a right-hand hitter just hit a foul ball over the first-base dugout, he is late on my fastball. That dictates my next pitch. I am going to stay with my fastball because he is late on it. I am sure not going to throw him a change up and speed up his bat.

Ken really opened up my eyes to pitching one pitch at a time. Playing that way is so simple in theory, but so very hard to actually do. Ken also talked about the signal lights.

## MIND CONTROL IS KEY

The game of baseball has superstition engrained throughout. It is a weird thing, but you often find yourself having negative thoughts at random times for no particular reason. It's almost like you are psyching yourself out to not have negative thoughts so much that you have more negative thoughts because you are trying to block them out. It's crazy.

I remember Ken said to not think about a pink elephant and that is all I could think about for the next twenty minutes.

Baseball is designed to make you think. If you go out and you have a good inning, your reward is to come back in and sit on the bench. If your team is hitting well and you hit for 20 minutes, you can start over-analyzing and thinking to yourself about things that you just shouldn't be thinking about.

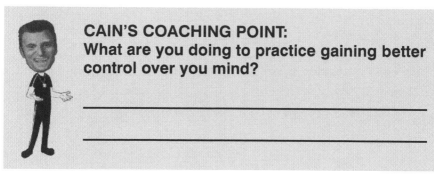

**CAIN'S COACHING POINT:**
**What are you doing to practice gaining better control over you mind?**

_____

_____

**Check out the Brian Cain Peak Performance Podcast and Brian Cain APP for the iPhone to get free mental conditioning training tools.**

## HAVE A RELEASE, THE ETCH-A-SKETCH MENTALITY

Those negative thoughts are red lights and you have to recognize these red light thoughts and have a release to let them go so you can get back to green. Before I met Ken I had no release and no physical way to let go of the negative thoughts. Now I accept them for what they are, let them pass and lock in on my focal point, take a good deep breath and refocus on what I am trying to do in that specific moment.

The best analogy that comes to my mind is that of an Etch-A-Sketch. Whatever comes to your mind, if negative, shake it up, clear the screen and start over.

## RECOGNIZE – RELEASE - REFOCUS

When you are driving a car and you come to a green light you go. There is not a lot of thought process that goes into it. In baseball when you are pitching and you have confident thoughts or you are feeling good and have positive self-talk, that's a green light. When you have green lights, you get the ball back from the catcher, get on the mound and go.

If you are driving a car and come to a yellow light, you must slow down at the intersection, or speed up. Regardless, you must process the information and make a decision.

In baseball, when players get into yellow lights, they will often speed up and put themselves into red lights and beat themselves. When you are driving a car and come to a red light, you must stop or you are going to crash and burn. You might survive one run through a red light, but eventually, you will crash and burn.

Run through enough yellow lights behind the wheel and you are going to get in a car accident as well. Ken's signal light analogy applies to baseball as well and especially to pitching.

If a guy who got a hit off me the last time comes to the plate and I think "Oh, no, this guy got a hit off me last time," that thought is a yellow light. You have to approach every situation with a controlled aggressiveness and rage, a relaxed intensity and humble confidence that says, "Okay, yeah. This guy got a hit off me last time. So what, that is in the past. I'm going to get him out this time."

**CAIN'S COACHING POINT:**
**What is your physical release when you get into red lights?**

_____

_____

## CHECK THE REARVIEW MIRROR

Check your rearview mirror as that hitter comes to the plate again. What did you throw him the last time? Did I make a mistake or did he hammer one of my quality pitches? Did I beat myself or did he beat me? Did I hang a curve ball or throw a fastball right down the middle? You can learn something from every hitter. You may find that when you go back and evaluate, there's nothing wrong with your approach or performance, that's when you tip your hat and you say, "It was out of my control. I executed, and you won."

You are going to lose in this game. If you don't, there is a plaque waiting for you in Cooperstown or you are a grown man competing against little leaguers and the competition has not caught up to you yet.

## ITCHING TO GO AND AWARE

How many times do you pull up to an intersection with a red light and you're itching to go? Be itching to go when that red light comes, never be tentative. Be itching to go, and be aware. Check oncoming traffic and know what's coming up behind you. Be ready for the green light because, when it comes, you want to punch the gas and be ultra aggressive. There is no place in baseball for being passive.

## HOW TO WORK WITH UMPIRES

I see too many players and coaches that let umpires take them out of their games. If you ever let an umpire dictate anything, you are crazy. Just mentioning the word umpire means you are in a red light. An umpire is a human being that's put behind home plate. And who knows what his experience is? Who knows if he has a grudge or is hungover. Whatever. You have no control of the umpire. He is there to do his job, you focus on doing yours. He may cause you to make an adjustment and baseball is a game of adjustments, so what. As soon as you start to let an umpire dictate what you do, that is a major red light. Recognize it, release it and refocus. If your focus becomes the umpire rather than your dynamic balance, extension and aggressive execution, you are letting a factor outside of your control defeat you. You are defeating yourself.

**CAIN'S COACHING POINT:**
**When have you let an umpire or an official take you out of your game? What would you do differently if that same situation happened today?**

_____

_____

## KNOW THE STRIKE ZONE

There is a rule book in baseball and there is a strike zone defined in the rule book. Tear it out and throw it out the window. Rip that page out of your rule book because the strike zone is wearing blue behind home plate, it is human and it is whatever the umpire says it is that day. As soon as you start to understand that, refuse to argue with him and only show confidence and aggressive body language on the mound, you increase your chances of executing your pitches, and increase your chances to win.

## BASEBALL IS 90% MENTAL

People always say that baseball is 90% mental, yet we work on it less than 10% of the time. By working on my mental game and becoming more aware of my thoughts and actions on the mound I really think I have extended my career a few years at least. I have gone from a classic primal pitcher who tried to throw as hard as he could each pitch to trying to make things move as much as I could and really having a purpose for each pitch. I think I've become a more complete pitcher at this point in my career, and the mental game has no doubt helped my longevity.

## NOT ENOUGH EMPHASIS
## PLACED ON MENTAL GAME

Unfortunately, at the college and professional levels, where baseball really becomes a mental game, I think there is not nearly enough emphasis placed on how to condition yourself mentally for success. Most coaches think working harder builds mental toughness. Working harder with the wrong mentality makes you mentally weak that much faster because you are training and engraining the wrong thought process.

## FIRST MAJOR LEAGUE SPRING TRAINING OUTING

I remember my first Major League Spring Training outing and we were playing the LA Angels in Tempe, Arizona. I was in the bullpen and the phone rang. "Get Cameron going," they said.

There was a man on first with one out, and I am throwing the ball as hard as I can for 15 minutes in the bullpen. It was like 90 degrees, I am sweating buckets, breathing heavy, and Todd Jones, closer for the Rockies comes over and says, "Cam, What are you doing?" I did not hear him so he says, "Hey, kid. What are you doing?"

"Well, I'm getting ready to go in."

He says, "There's two outs with a runner on first and an 0-2 count. Why are you throwing fastballs as hard as you can, rapid fire? You are probably not going to go in the game. Look at the situation. He's one pitch away from getting out of the inning."

At that point it just kind of hit me. We then talked about what it means to get loose and get ready when you play 162 games in a season. Getting ready doesn't have to be this all-out max effort. I was not aware of the situation and was in red lights.

A few years later I am playing in Venezuela, and we had a few guys who were 20 or 21 and right out of rookie ball. They were in the pen warming up and throwing 100 miles an hour in the bullpen for a half-hour. It was 100 degrees. They were burning themselves out in the heat. They needed to step back and look at the situation and say, "Hey, two outs, two-strike count, nobody on. I'm going to hold off on warming up." You have to be aware. ***Awareness is the first step to accomplishment***. I think you could call the mental game the awareness game and be just as accurate.

## AWARENESS GAME VS. MENTAL GAME

The mental game is really the awareness game. I think when you say mental game, it turns some guys off because they think of school and sitting in a classroom and some guys just hated doing that. When you talk about the aware game and what's going on inside of the game and inside of yourself, you have a much better chance of getting through to a professional baseball player and any athlete, really.

How many times do you see a pitcher go down to the bullpen to get loose and they don't have any clue as to what is going on in the game. Their focus is on getting loose and they end up throwing way too many pitches in the bullpen. You don't want to blow all of your bullets in the pen. Todd Jones taught me that. Now, when I get loose I understand that I still have eight pitches to get on the mound, so if I get called in the ball game I still have eight pitches. My goal in the pen is to get my body warm and loose and get a little sweat going, but it should not be 100% effort unless I know I am going to go into the game.

I have the eight pitches in the game and the slow walk and long talk by the manager which can get me another five to eight in the bullpen. You have almost 16 pitches to be ready to go. You have to trust that those pitches are going to get you ready to compete. The worst thing you can do is get hot, then sit and repeat that process day in and day out.

## THE TALENT PYRAMID

As you get higher and higher in the levels of competition, physical talent means less and less because in order to get to that higher level, everyone has talent. The talent pyramid shows that when you get to the top of the pyramid, talent's irrelevant and it becomes a game of consistency. It becomes about catching a break and all the intangibles that you have no control over, such as politics of the organization, can play a role, but you must go out and play hard every day, put up numbers, and trust your stuff.

## ADVICE FOR COACHES

If I had a message to deliver to coaches through my experience, it would be to throw the cookie cutter out the window. Embrace the individuality that each player you have brings to your team because that's what's going to make your team successful. It's what each guy brings to the table. Everybody would love to cut Alex Rodriguez out or Derek Jeter out and have nine of them, but that is not going to happen.

Each guy you have right now, no matter how good or how bad, brings something to the table. Look at Rudy Ruettiger, he brought something to the table at Notre Dame that brought the team together. Every guy wanted to put his jersey on the table because Rudy represented what it meant to be a part of Notre Dame football. On every team there are those guys that are a critical part of the puzzle but may not look the role or have the physical gifts that scream big league talent.

Embrace diversity. Embrace individuality. And love it because it will help you to win.

## ADVICE FOR PLAYERS

My advice for players is to work hard, be aggressive, trust your abilities and understand what your abilities are so that as you develop more physically and mentally you will find that the game will become simpler.

The mental game provides you with tools that are going to help you improve as a player and as a person. If you continue to have the drive and motivation, continue to be aggressive, trust yourself and you keep your eyes and ears open the whole time, you are going to get the most out of your abilities. Be sure that you get it done in the classroom as well because the odds are not in your favor that you will make a living playing baseball or any sport. Get an education, play hard and have fun. Being an athlete should be one of the most fun times in your life.

You can contact Ryan at ragarm29@yahoo.com.

# CHAPTER #8 REVIEW

☐ **What is the mental game**

☐ **Adversity is essential**

☐ **Two paces to the game**

☐ **Know game situation – each pitch has a purpose**

☐ **Awareness of what is working**

☐ **Check points**

☐ **Awareness and control**

☐ **The speed of baseball**

☐ **Practice controlling the pace**

☐ **Horror movies tell all**

☐ **What to do with the scared player**

☐ **Evaluate good and bad, be aggressive**

☐ **Throwing strikes is not enough**

☐ **Put yourself in the scary situation**

☐ **Humble confidence**

☐ **Balance, extension, aggressive execution**

☐ **The law of average**

☐ **Learn from everyone**

☐ **Greg Maddux got it**

☐ **Perfection is Satan**

☐ **You can not make up for the past**

☐ **Be a student of the game**

☐ **Take advantage of opportunities**

☐ **Different approach from amateur to pro**

☐ **Tewks shares his experience**

- [ ] Meeting the master of the mental game
- [ ] One pitch at a time
- [ ] Mind control is key
- [ ] Have a release , the etch-a-sketch mentality
- [ ] Recognize – release - refocus
- [ ] Check the rearview mirror
- [ ] Itching to go and aware
- [ ] How to work with umpires
- [ ] Know the strike zone
- [ ] Baseball is 90% mental
- [ ] First major league spring training outing
- [ ] Awareness game vs. Mental game
- [ ] The talent pyramid
- [ ] Advice for coaches
- [ ] Advice for players

# CHAPTER #9

## AMANDA CRABTREE, SOFTBALL PITCHER USES MENTAL GAME TO TURN CAREER AROUND & LEADS COUNTRY IN STRIKEOUTS PER GAME

*A*manda Crabtree was one of the top pitchers in all of college softball during the 2011 season. She led the country in strikeouts per seven innings and led her team to one game from the NCAA Women's College World Series and to one of the best seasons in history at The University of Houston. She discusses how the mental game made a difference for her on and off the diamond and was the missing piece of her performance puzzle.

*Crabtree grew up in Kingwood, Texas, and went to Kingwood High School where she played all four years on the school's varsity softball team. She also played on a top select team out of Houston as well as participated in high school volleyball her freshman year.*

### WHEN TO FOCUS ON ONE SPORT

I knew that softball was my sport and would be the sport that I could play in college so I started focusing on just playing softball after my freshman year of high school because that specialization would give me the best chance to play in college. I started getting recruited at the end of my freshman year and started getting contacted by college coaches through emails to my coaches.

## FINDING THE COLLEGE OF YOUR CHOICE

I decided to go to Oklahoma State. My parents were really supportive of whatever I wanted do and that was the best thing that I think parents can do, support the decision that your son or daughter makes in where they want to pursue their college education. There were definitely some things that I was looking for in schools.

Going into college athletics from high school, you do not always know what you are getting yourself into and I am not sure you can ever be totally prepared for the jump from high school to college in any sport. All you can do is make the best decision based on all the information you have at the time, trust your gut and go with it. I chose Oklahoma State. I loved Stillwater, Oklahoma where the school is and I loved the traditions. I loved everything about the school and the program.

## COLLEGE SPORTS CAN BE A RUDE AWAKENING

When I got to Oklahoma State for my freshman year, things did not go as expected. It was a lot harder for me to be away from home than I had expected. I was dealing with injuries for the first time in my career and that was a major stressor for me. Freshman year was a big wakeup call. I give pitching lessons now, and I always tell my students that college softball is a lot different than what you think of high school softball and even competitive travel softball. It's a huge step up in competition and I do not think my mind was prepared for that level of softball.

## FAILS FOR FIRST TIME

It was the first time that I had faced a lot of adversity and I was not prepared to deal with it. I had not developed the skill set yet to embrace adversity and did not see adversity as a part of the growth process that is necessary and required to take your game to the next level. I saw myself as a failure.

It was really, really tough on me. I had a lot of doubts about myself and my talent. I struggled a lot with whether or not I should even keep playing. My parents and I had a lot of late night phone calls and discussions about my future in softball.

I had lost my love for the game and figured I needed to try to find a place to play closer to home. So, I was back at "square one" being recruited again and ended up at The University of Houston, who had recruited me out of high school.

## FRESH START, SAME CHALLENGES

I was excited for a fresh start. I transferred my sophomore year and it felt like my freshman year all over. I was brand new to the program, did not know anyone and felt like I was still falling short of my potential. I was expecting everything to change and nothing changed for me. I started to doubt myself again. I was putting in all the work, working as hard as I possibly could, maybe too hard at times and just was not getting the results that I felt I should be getting. My sophomore year was pretty miserable.

## ANOTHER YEAR, ANOTHER STRUGGLE

Junior year got a little bit better but I didn't really meet any of the goals I set for myself. I lost my confidence and my focus on the process in games most of the time and kept getting disappointed with myself. I was thinking about quitting; the game was just not fun for me anymore.

## KEY TO UNLOCKING POTENTIAL IS FOUND

When my senior year came along our coach, Kyla Holas, had a mental conditioning coach, Brian Cain, come and work with our team and staff. The three days we spent together as a team were eye opening for me. I think it was a combination of Coach Holas teaching me about the process and the way that Cain conveyed some of the same concepts, but it just started to make sense to me.

## UNIQUE STYLE – FINDING OUT
## WHO YOU NEED TO BE

I always thought I was supposed to be a the stoic, unemotional pitcher who was ultra-aggressive and might even cursing at a batter and be fired up with competitiveness to beat you. I tried to make myself that pitcher and it did not work for me. I am a very realistic person who is comfortable in my own skin and just being me. I pitch with my emotions on my sleeve, and those emotions are usually a big smile or laugh because I love playing softball and don't feel like I need to get fired up or make it personal between me and the hitter. I had always thought that my true personality was a weakness of mine in competition and never really had people who embraced that style around me, but once I learned I could just be me, I had a lot more success.

## AH HA MOMENT

I remember having a conversation one day with Cain when I asked, "Do you think that it's weird that when I get kind of stressed out during a game I stop and pray?"

Then Cain said, "You know, you are not the only pitcher that does that. There are closers in Major League Baseball that will go out to the mound and know that the result is out of their control. They say it is in God's hands and that they just execute a pitch and let the outcome take care of itself. Whatever works for you, works for you."

And from that moment on a light bulb went off and I realized that what I had been doing, trying to be a pitcher that showed no emotion and was stoic and tough was just not who I needed to be to have success.

I had been trying to fit this mold of somebody else, and it made me miserable. I started to do the things that I used to do and made the game fun again. Next thing you know, I was getting the results I always wanted and having a lot more fun in the process.

It was a big transition in the way that I thought, the way that I performed and the way that I practiced. I was having so much fun just playing the game of softball as if it was a game and not life and death. I realized that my self-worth was not tied up in how well I pitched, but that I was two separate people. Who I was as an athlete and who I was as a person. Softball was not who I was, it was what I did, and that approach made the game a lot more fun and turned all the pressure I had felt into pleasure.

## REGRETS & EXPENSIVE EXPERIENCE

It makes me so sad, sometimes, that it took me three years of being miserable to figure out that I should not be treating the game like it was life and death, *that I needed to have fun to play well and not just have fun when I played well*.

## TALENT IS OVERRATED

I went from being a pitcher who struggled for three years to leading the country in strikeouts per seven innings pitched and was in the top two or three pitchers in the country in hits given up per seven innings. I felt like I was finally having the success I had worked so hard for and the success that my ability and the quality of the coaching I had received should have allowed me to have.

Physical talent is never enough. You can have tremendous physical talent, but if you don't think the right way or you're not having fun and you're putting more pressure than you need to on yourself to be perfect, you're not going to have success.

I had all of the tools. I always tell people that I was no better as a pitcher in my senior year of college than I was my first three. I simply got my head screwed on straight. Literally, my pitches did not get any better. I didn't suddenly develop three new pitches that were fantastic or out of this world. I had the same pitches that were good every other year, but all of a sudden I learned to control the six inches between my ears where it used to control me.

## ANALYSIS PARALYSIS

I am a very big analyzer. I analyze everything to death, which is a good trait to have as a pitcher, if you can keep it under control. I analyze to paralysis.

I used to get scouting reports and it would paralyze me because I would be thinking so much about the report and who was on deck and what I was supposed to throw that I could not keep my focus in the moment and on playing this pitch, and to be successful in softball you must go one pitch at a time.

## PERFECTIONISM KILLS PERFORMANCE

I was a perfectionist. I had to be perfect no matter what and so I became a checklist pitcher. I always had a checklist that I had to do for each pitch and I let that over-analysis, in an attempt to be perfect in an imperfect game, affect my pace.

When I was stressed out or when I was mad at myself, I would not breathe and refocus between pitches. I didn't ever take time to check in on my signal lights or my breathing; I just got the ball and started thinking. All of that thinking really slowed down my pace and zapped me of my confidence and belief.

## ROUTINE HELPS SET PACE

I really had no mental game routine. I tried to repeat my mechanics physically, but always rushed physically because I was rushing mentally. I was playing three, four, sometimes five pitches ahead instead of going one pitch at a time.

I really worked on a routine and my breathing each pitch in the fall before my senior year and I think that was a big game changer for me. The people who played against me my senior year really hated hitting off me because I took my time and had a slower pace than most pitchers, but it was the exact pace I needed to pitch my best.

I always tried to have a fast pace and should have worked to find the right pace. The pace of my new, slower routine worked for me. I took my time. I would always go to the back of the mound and visualize the last pitch I threw, but it going exactly where I wanted it to go. I always took a huge breath and just let all of the stress that I would put on myself go.

## CHANGE SELF TALK, CHANGE YOUR LIFE

The main thing that changed for me was the way that I talked to myself. I used to analyze everything to death. Even a good pitch, I would find something wrong with it. When I finally realized that as a pitcher you have the odds in your favor, and all you need to do is just make quality pitches, my whole game changed.

I learned that no pitcher is perfect. Sometimes, you throw flat rise balls, you throw curve balls that hang. I would just say, "OK. That pitch is gone, nothing I can do about it now, let's just move on with the next one." Prior to my senior year, I would've been very disappointed in myself. And I would've had so much stress on me that the negative spiral would have continued. I would have taken that yellow light of a poor pitch and it would have immediately snowballed into a red light.

## GREEN SHOELACES

As the game went on, normally, the stress got greater and greater for me. Before my senior year, I never had a way to let the stress go personally, and neither did we as a team.

One of the ways our team helped each other get to the next pitch was to have everyone wear one green shoelace. The green shoelace was important because when the game started to speed up on me, and I was not performing well, like most athletes, one of the first things that would happen was that my head would go down. Now when my head went down, I would see the green shoelace and it reminded me to get to the next pitch.

## USE THE SHOELACE AS A RELEASE

When the game sped up on me and I needed to stop and slow it down, I would step out of the circle, call time out and retie my shoe. This physical pause would help me to take a mental pause and I felt like it removed me from the situation, allowed me to flush everything that had happened in the past, and get my mind and body back to where I needed to be in the present.

Sometimes, the other team would get frustrated and I am sure my teammates may have as well because I might tie my shoes as many as three times in an inning if I was struggling, and they knew that nothing was coming untied. However, that release of untying my shoes really helped me stay in a positive and green light mindset.

I think many athletes perform well when they are talking negative to themselves. One of my biggest challenges was always quieting the voice of negativity that would show up in competition. I needed to have a physical release to stop and reset myself when I started to spiral out of control.

## SENIOR YEAR = TOTALLY DIFFERENT PITCHER

I was a totally different pitcher my senior year and I think it was largely due to me changing everything except for my pitching. I changed my routine. I changed my self-talk. I changed how seriously I took myself, I changed almost everything mentally and hardly anything physically, if anything at all.

Before my senior year, if I pitched badly, I thought that I was a bad person. I didn't separate softball from real life. Softball was who I was, not what I did. When I started to separate who I was as a competitor and who I was as a person, it really wasn't such a big deal to have a bad day at the field anymore because I did not take it with me to my personal life, and this really helped me to minimize my poor performance streaks because every day was a new day versus everyday being life and death. I was able to have a bad day and say, "OK, let's move on, and let's do better the next time."

## SEPARATING LIFE AS PERSON AND COMPETITOR

A big mistake that athletes make is they look at softball as who they are, not what they do. And they live and die with every pitch and live and die with every game. When you can separate yourself from the game and see yourself and your self-worth as a human being not tied up in your performance, you're going to perform better. A lot of players have a pre-practice routine they use to get locked into being a softball player and a post-practice they use to let go of being a softball player. I didn't necessarily have anything that you would've seen.

A lot of my teammates used the changing of their clothes as a way to help separate from softball to their real self. When the uniform was on, they were the softball player, when it was off they were the student. For me, it was more of a mental attitude shift when I put my cleats on, I put on my softball attitude. And then when I took them off, I put on my real-world attitude.

## SOFTBALL IS NOT LIFE AND DEATH

I think that when most athletes are not happy with their performance on a consistent basis, this happens because they are living and dying by their successes on the field. I can personally say that I lived my first three years of college determining my self-worth by how my softball went.

A lot of athletes make the mistake of personalizing performance and seeing their self-worth wrapped up in how they perform in sport. It happens a lot I think because as a college athlete, you put so much of yourself into your sport and into what you do that you take that success and failure very personal. As with a lot of things we've talked about, personalizing performance can be good and bad. There's nothing in life that's good or bad. It's always good *and* bad. And personalizing that performance is good in the sense that it's going to motivate you to work harder and to do better. However, when you get to a certain level of competition, for me it was college softball, being the perfectionist and personalizing performance zaps you of any confidence that you might have because you are going to struggle, at some point, when you play against the best players in the country. If you are a perfectionist or evaluate as good or bad and fail to accept that you should evaluate as good *and* bad, you end up beating yourself.

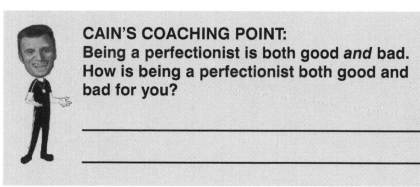

**CAIN'S COACHING POINT:**
Being a perfectionist is both good *and* bad. How is being a perfectionist both good and bad for you?

_____

_____

## THE PERFECTIONIST TEST

My senior year we won the NCAA Regional at The University of Texas and went to Oklahoma State for the NCAA Super Regional. Coach Holas noticed that we were tight before the game and had us all step inside of a bucket with water to prove that we could not walk on water. Her point was taken and we loosened up immediately.

**www.BrianCain.com/experience For BONUS Mental Conditioning Material & To See The Video of Coach Holas Taking The Team Through The Perfectionist Test.**

When you are putting in 20-40 hours a week practicing, it feels like you should be perfect. And having us try to walk on water, as elementary as it sounds, was a great way to reinforce this point rather than just talking about it.

Every single person is going to make mistakes throughout this journey, and that's ok, it is all about how you respond to those mistakes that defines who you are and who you become. Prior to walking on water, I think everybody was tense. It was a big game. It was the second time the University of Houston had ever been to super-regionals and her test to walk on water really helped to settle our nerves and refocused us on playing our game and playing pitch to pitch.

## FOCAL POINTS HELP TO REFOCUS

When I would get stressed, an umpire would miss a call, a teammate would make an error or if I was doubting myself or not having the positive self-talk, those little things used to be big things to me. Finding a focal point was a critical part of my being able to release those negatives and refocus on going one pitch at a time.

During the game I would turn around and focus on a needle on the top of a building in deep center field. That needle was my focal point and the place I looked when I needed to release my red lights and get back into green.

That needle worked better for me as a focal point than the second base bag or a foul pole would have. I liked it because it was far away from softball. I was looking at downtown Houston, of all these massive buildings made of glass and metal, and I was playing on this great manicured dirt and grass. It was a polar opposite and gave me that, "OK. This is just a game. There's more to life, this is not life" feeling and it would ground me.

I would look at my focal point, wipe the chalk off the back of the pitchers circle and say, "OK. It's done. I'm moving on. Next Pitch!" I always thought that when I turned around and faced the batter again that it was done. It was in the past, there was nothing I could do about it anymore. All I could do was pitch the next pitch.

This release and the focal point gave me a systematic way to constantly release the little things that irritate you over the course of a game and can go from being a small nag into a big problem if you let them.

If I didn't agree with the umpire's call or if I was in red lights, I would go to my focal point and release. If I was having a bad game, I might do this a hundred times that game. Most games, I may have only looked at it twice. My focal point gave me a way where people didn't really know what I was doing, to give me peace of mind and get me back in that green light mentality, and it really helped. The release and the focal point gave me a way to stop and slow down rather than trying to work faster, which is what a lot of people do and that never helped me, and I don't think helps very many people.

## SPORT SPECIALIZATION

Recruiting for college athletics has gone from finding the best juniors and seniors in high school to the best seventh and eighth graders in the country. Even though this is the case for the best 1% of players in the country, I always encourage young people to play just about every sport under the sun growing up. I swam for a long time and played softball, soccer, volleyball, basketball, and also ran track and danced.

I knew that when I chose softball, it was the one sport that I really wanted to choose. I think some athletes that specialize in one sport quit other sports too soon and always wonder if they had just played a little longer, what would have happened?

My advice to younger athletes is to always try as many sports as you can because you may think that you like one sport and you're going to try another sport, and you might like it better.

There may come a time where you realize that you love one sport and are just going to play that sport. I kind of whittled my sports down until I really knew, confidently, that softball was what I wanted to put all of my time and effort into. When you're starting to get recruited by colleges, you're going to have to make up your mind because I think if you want to do yourself justice and find the best fit for yourself, you do have to specialize in one sport, especially if you're a pitcher. I think if you play other positions you have a little bit more flexibility. But softball pitching is so demanding that I think you have to choose early or you will be behind the competition.

That was the challenge I was faced with. I couldn't play club volleyball, high school volleyball, travel softball and high school softball and be good at them all. That is what I wanted, to do them all, but I had to make a choice.

## DO YOU PICK SPORT, OR DOES SPORT PICK YOU?

Sometimes you get to pick when you want to specialize and other times, the sport kind of makes that choice for you. It may depend on where you live and how competitive the sports are in your area or it may depend on what sport you want to play at the next level.

Sometimes, your sport's going to dictate that you commit full-time, but if you are young, my message is get involved early in as many sports as you can and then stay involved in the ones that you love until it's time, if you want to play in college, for you to specialize. If you don't want to play in college, then maybe you don't need to specialize.

## MENTAL IMAGERY PLAYS LARGE ROLE IN PREPARATION

I always struggled with self-confidence, especially after the first three years that I had. I had a lot of self-doubt. I had never struggled in softball until I got to college, so failure was something that I just didn't really know how to deal with.

My senior year, I dedicated myself to using mental imagery as a part of my preparation routine. I would sit down when there were two outs, find a spot on the bench by myself, close my eyes, and go through the warm-ups that I was about to go and throw on the mound.

Every inning, I had the same warm-up routine.

1. Curve out
2. Curve in
3. Rise
4. Drop out
5. Screw
6. Curve out

I would visualize myself throwing the most amazing curve ball, outside, I'd ever thrown. I'd go through all the pitches I was going to throw in my warm ups and I would throw them the best I had ever thrown them. Then, when I walked out onto the mound, I already had six awesome pitches under my belt. And then all those pitches in warm-ups just built on top of each other and my confidence would grow from there.

It was a really good way for me to stay in touch with the game. Pitchers can sometimes get lethargic in the dugout, especially during a long inning, and your mind can start to kind of wander. Using mental imagery in the dugout was a really good way for me not to lose anything. It was a way for me to see good pitches in my mind, feel them in my body and I didn't have to tire my arms or my body out by throwing them.

Doing mental imagery of those warm up pitches was an important part of my routine that got me mentally ready for the inning that was I going into, but it also gave me that little boost of confidence. Even though I didn't throw a pitch, I walked out there feeling like all my pitches were on.

## RECOGNIZING YOUR SIGNAL LIGHTS

I think one of the biggest challenges athletes have is recognizing when they're out of that green light mentality and are getting into yellow or red so they can recognize they are starting to lose it so they can change their thought process, stop the bleeding, and turn it around, one pitch at a time.

Recognizing my signal lights was something that was a challenge for me at first. I worked on recognizing my signal lights with my pitching coach Abbie Simms a lot that fall. She was really good at being like, "OK, Amanda, you're getting a little bit crazy right now, step off and release." She would just say enough where I would be like, "Oh, you're right. I'm kind of rushing right now. I'm not doing a very good job of going pitch to pitch." She started pointing out some things and then it made me more aware.

## AWARENESS IS THE FIRST STEP
## TO ACCOMPLISHMENT

I became so in tune with the way that my body worked that whenever I was feeling stressed, I literally could feel the heat drive through my body. It was crazy. It was like I could feel my blood boiling when I got into red lights and it allowed me to recognize, release and refocus on the next pitch.

When my mind was good and I was in green lights, my thoughts were slow and clear. When I would get frustrated or things were starting to spin out of control, my thoughts would start to race.

**CAIN'S COACHING POINT:**
Start to gain an awareness of when you perform at your best and when you perform at your worst so that you can better recognize when you are beating yourself and turn it around by changing your self-talk, releasing your negative thoughts and getting back into the present moment.

**WHEN AT MY BEST (GREEN) I WOULD DESCRIBE MY:**

**THOUGHTS/SELF-TALK:**

_____

_____

**PHYSICAL FEELINGS:**

_____

_____

**WHEN AT MY WORST (RED) I WOULD DESCRIBE MY:**

**THOUGHTS/SELF-TALK:**

_____

_____

**PHYSICAL FEELINGS:**

_____

_____

Becoming aware of my thoughts and feelings took a lot of practice. Every day, I had to check in on my thoughts and feelings when I was pitching. It also helped that I really trusted Abbie and I knew she wasn't just going to say, "Hey, Amanda. You're getting crazy," when I wasn't. She wanted me to figure it out on my own and asked me a lot of questions, which helped to build my self-awareness.

Finding somebody that you can trust and who can see you when you start to get into red lights is key. Our third baseman would sometimes come over and just talk to me for a second because she could tell that I was just a little bit out of my rhythm and it would slow me back down and help me get back into the rhythm I needed to pitch my best.

I think if you really work together as a team, you start to learn when people are totally out of whack. And if they're not realizing, there's somebody on the team that can go up and be like, "Hey. You need to tie your shoe" and it will be ok because that relationship has been established and you trust their words.

## SO WHAT NEXT PITCH MENTALITY

I was a big over-thinker; I am a big planner. In softball though, you can't plan anything other than the pitch you are about to throw. I used to think about what I was going to do 3, 4, 5 pitches from now and I would get so far away from the present moment and this pitch that I beat myself.

There would be times my first three years where if they got a runner on base I would be thinking, "Oh my gosh. If this next person gets on and then I walk the next person, the bases are going to be loaded and then I'm going to give up a grand slam."

That's how I would think. Once I learned the "so what, next pitch" mentality and started to really understand what it meant to play one pitch at a time, all of sudden, pitching and handling the stress that comes with pitching was much easier.

It was so much easier to let all those things go. It was so much easier to think about the game because all you were thinking about was one thing at a time. Again, it takes a lot of time and team building to get there, but once you know each other, it becomes a part of your culture and part of how you talk with each other. "So what, next pitch" is all you can say at certain times. "So what" means you acknowledge that the result was not what you wanted and that there is NOTHING you can do at this present moment about the past. "Next pitch" gives you the right thing to focus on, playing and winning the next pitch.

## MENTAL GAME EXTENDS INTO LIFE AFTER SOFTBALL

Everything that I have learned in the mental game of softball I still use every day in my life after softball. I am a kindergarten teacher and use the skills I learned through the mental game of softball in my life every day. I teach my five-year-old kindergartners how to use the same skills every single day. Skills like not counting the days, but making the days count have been huge for me as a teacher.

## ANTIDOTE FOR THE GRIND OF EVERYDAY WORK

I, like most people, get in the mindset where you're working and it's like, "Oh, another day at work. Oh, another day at work. Oh, another day at work." and you kind of lose that wow factor and the excitement that you had when you first got hired.

Especially being a teacher, you can lose the awe of being a teacher. I wanted to be a teacher for the longest time. I think it's the absolute coolest job there is and you put so much of yourself into what you do that there are times where you get really tired. You're worn down. Having the mental skills like a "compared to what" perspective or to recognize when you are in red lights versus green lights and having routines helps you to bring the energy and commitment to excellence that you need to bring everyday and that your students deserve.

## DOMINATE THE DAY

I wake up every day with the goal to dominate the day. I try to make every day the best day I have ever had in the classroom. Teaching kids can be exhausting. It can be a handful, especially when they don't listen, which is most of the time.

Having releases and a way to let go of the negative emotion and frustration has been huge. I may get frustrated during the day, but I can't show them I'm frustrated. So I have to come up with a way to let those emotions go because it's not a five-year-old's fault. Just like it's not softball's fault.

I think the way that I learned to deal with the stress and pressure of softball prepared me better than anything else for real life: a career. Stopping to take a breath has been one of the most beneficial skills I have taken from softball to the classroom.

## SPORT DOES NOT DEFINE YOU

Softball does not define you as a person because the moment that you really understand that you are not your performance, everything that you do is going to get better. No one thing in your life defines you. I think that too many people and too many athletes don't realize that your career or your sport does not define who you really are. I wish I had learned that a lot earlier in my career.

You can contact Amanda Crabtree by email at abcrabtree27@yahoo.com.

# ̃IAPTER #9 REVIEW

- [ ] When to focus on one sport
- [ ] Finding the college of your choice
- [ ] College sports can be a rude awakening
- [ ] Fails for first time
- [ ] Fresh start, same challenges
- [ ] Another year, another struggle
- [ ] Key to unlocking potential is found
- [ ] Unique style – finding out who you need to be
- [ ] Ah ha moment
- [ ] Regrets & expensive experience
- [ ] Talent is overrated
- [ ] Analysis paralysis
- [ ] Perfectionism kills performance
- [ ] Routine helps set pace
- [ ] Change self-talk, change your life
- [ ] Green shoelaces
- [ ] Use the shoelace as a release
- [ ] Senior year = totally different pitcher
- [ ] Separating life as person and competitor
- [ ] Softball is not life and death
- [ ] The perfectionist test
- [ ] Focal points help to refocus
- [ ] Sport specialization
- [ ] Do you pick sport, or does sport pick you?
- [ ] Mental imagery plays large role in preparation

- [ ] Recognizing your signal lights
- [ ] Awareness is the first step to accomplishment
- [ ] So what, next pitch mentality
- [ ] Mental game extends into life after softball
- [ ] Antidote for the grind of everyday work
- [ ] Dominate the day
- [ ] Sport does not define you

# CHAPTER #10

## MIKE SPILLANE, HOCKEY GOALIE, USES MENTAL GAME TO EMBRACE ADVERSITY & PLAY HIS BEST HOCKEY

*Michael Spillane played goalie for the University of Vermont from 2006-2009. He is currently playing with the Arizona Sundogs of the Central Hockey League. Spillane discusses how mental conditioning has helped his on-ice performance and explains how he uses the skills that he has learned through hockey in his everyday life.*

### INEXPENSIVE EXPERIENCE AND GIVING BACK TO THE GAME

I am glad to have the chance to share how mental conditioning has been a huge part of my development as a goalie and as a person. When given the opportunity, I try to give back to the game by sharing my experiences with others to try and help them learn from my experience. Learning from others is what I call an inexpensive experience, while learning from your own trial and error is what I refer to as expensive experience.

To play this game at the highest level and to get the most out of your ability, you must constantly be seeking inexpensive experiences from others. You need to seek out those who are at the highest level and find out what they do to make themselves great and learn from their experiences to speed up your learning curve.

### REMAINING CALM IS ESSENTIAL

The most important thing is you have to know how to remain calm in pressure situations as a goalie, just like you do in any position, in any sport. Staying calm is about recognizing when you are getting in those danger areas of red and yellow lights, when the game starts to speed up on you.

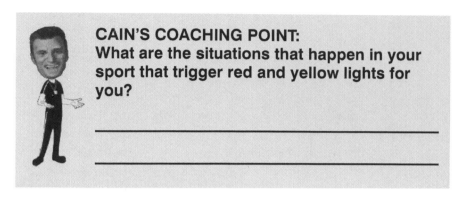

**CAIN'S COACHING POINT:**
**What are the situations that happen in your sport that trigger red and yellow lights for you?**

_____

_____

## ROUTINES ARE KEY FOR CONSISTENT PERFORMANCE

There is a lot that goes through your head while you are playing in a game as a goalie. You are on the ice for that full 60 minutes, there are a lot of ups and downs to the game, and you have to be able to find a routine both physically and mentally that works to keep you into playing one shift at a time.

Being able to take good deep breaths, and use positive self-talk and trigger words helps me to play with a relaxed intensity. I use this routine throughout the game as a part of my routine before each face off and I also have a routine for when the puck crosses the red line. I take another good deep breath and lock into the present moment.

The mental game has helped me to establish in-game routines that provide me with an effective system to deal with the constant ebb and flow of the game and to balance my emotions.

## EMOTIONAL BALANCE, RELAXED INTENSITY AND BREATHING

Breathing is the number one mental key for me. You want to play with a relaxed intensity. You want to be intense without being tense. The ability to take a good deep breath, when the puck comes across the red line, has made a huge difference for me.

There are so many thoughts that go through your head, and hockey is a long game if you do not allow yourself to space out and then use a routine to lock back in. You cannot stay engaged with the proper intensity that you need for a full 60 minutes. You must let your mind go and come back.

## FOCAL POINT: KEY PART OF ROUTINE

I take good, deep breaths while the puck is at the other end of the ice. I try to stay relaxed and then use a focal point after making saves or if there is a break in play. I look down at the top of the crease, where the blue and red paint come together, and take a good, deep breath and I snap back into the present moment immediately.

It is critical that you take good deep breaths and bring yourself back into the present moment because the routine of taking a breath on a focal point is the foundation of your pre-shift routine and it helps to form a consistency to your game where you feel like you lock in to this shift and are on top of your game. There is definitely not a better feeling than being completely into the present, having a quiet mind and strong body.

**CAIN'S COACHING POINT:**
**What is a focal point that you can go to and take a good deep breath on as a part of your routine?**

_____

_____

## PHYSICAL ABILITY IS IMPORTANT
## BUT NOT ENOUGH

When you are playing at the highest level of competition, talent becomes less and less important because everyone has it. When you are trying to be one of those few goalies that gets the chance to play in the National Hockey League, talent is a given. Everyone has talent. There are a lot of guys out there that have the ability to play the game at a high level and the difference maker is your ability to have consistency in performance. The best players do not always make it to the NHL. It is the guys who play the bestThe breath and the routine help you to be consistently at your best.

## ROUTINES, PRE-GAME, PRE-SHIFT, PRE-PERIOD

My routine has become very detailed and is a pretty extensive process that I go through to prepare. Not everyone is so "routine oriented" but for me I feel like having a routine is the best way for me to prepare for the game and the unexpected.

You have a routine that you go through to prepare, but if your routine gets messed up because of the unexpected, you do not freak out or panic. You just pick up your routine at the most opportune place, which may be as simple as walking from the locker room to the ice.

The process of having a routine has definitely changed my game in a positive way. Being able to lock in and space out in practice and on game days has been one of the most important skills I have developed. You cannot be locked in all the time. Your focus must ebb and flow like the pace of the game or you will burn yourself out. Having a routine you go through to get locked in is key.

I like to get to the rink a couple of hours early if it is a game day. The first hour is spent making sure I am relaxed and not doing too much over-thinking, letting my emotions get out of control, trying to be too perfect, hoping that things are going to work out.

I start with a solid stretch, followed by a shower where I warm my body up a little bit and let go of anything off the ice that I might be holding on to. I try to leave it in the shower and pick it up after the game.

After the shower, I go right to a foam roller to try to relax a little bit more. I also listen to my breathing and make sure that I am not tense whatsoever. I then put my iPod in and that is when I let my brain know it is time to lock in a little more with the mental focus. I use an iPod with certain songs I listen to that condition my mind to know that my body is about to go through a game on game days only. Having that separate iPod and music has really allowed me to lock in a lot easier and on a more consistent basis, while at the same time having that relaxed feeling, knowing that I am going to get it done.

I then do a dynamic warm-up and grab some tennis balls to do some juggling and some tracking of the spin on the ball and really try to see the seams on the tennis ball as they spin. I work to get my eyes moving well.

Once I am dressed and stretched out, right before I go on the ice, I just remind myself that I have performed and worked off the ice to perform and that I trust myself, my preparation and just go get it and let the game take care of itself because I know that I am going to perform at a certain standard of excellence.

My routine has become more detailed and more basic as I have gotten older and understand myself and the game of hockey more. I have really focused on working smarter instead of harder, which has definitely paid dividends. Working harder does not always work.

## IN GAME RELEASES

Having a release when you give up goals is key because you are going to give up goals; you cannot put up a shutout every night. What I do to release a goal, or to "flush it" so that I can get back to the next shift with a clear mind, is an important part of my in-game routine.

As a goalie, you are on the ice the whole time and when you give up a goal you have everybody telling you in the stands that you suck and calling you a "sieve." It is important that you recognize that you are not perfect, but are required to be excellent and must have a system to get you back to green lights after you give up a goal so you can attack that next shift with confidence and a clear mind.

The second the puck goes into the net, I get it out of the net as quickly as possible. I get out of the crease and will beat myself up. You have to have that moment of negativity and beat yourself up. I am a competitor, not a robot. I do this when I skate out of the crease towards the boards. When I turn my back to the cage and skate to the boards, that is my time to have negative self-talk, negative energy. When I come back into the crease, it is relentless, positive energy, and I am ready to play that next shift.

When I get back to the crease, I wipe whatever snow is around the top of the crease around the outside of the net and then I grab some water, I drink it, and I spray a bunch on my face to just help relax me. And then once my helmet comes back down, I go back to my focal point of the blue and red lines and take a really nice, big, deep breath and say, "So what, next shot!"

## CONFIDENCE IS A CHOICE

As a goalie, you are going to get scored on. You cannot let giving up a goal affect your performance on the next shift. Having a release routine helps you to stay confident and ready to make that next save on the next shot.

There are big moments in a game where you might give up goals as well and there are also big moments where you need to be able to focus on that next shot. If you let that one goal you give up eat at you, one can turn into three quite quickly playing this position. You must always remember that confidence is a choice and that you choose your body language and the words you say to yourself.

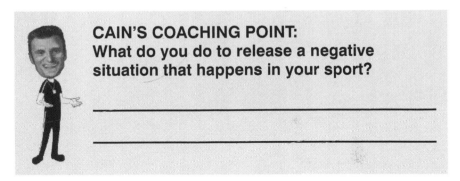

**CAIN'S COACHING POINT:**
**What do you do to release a negative situation that happens in your sport?**

_____

_____

## POST-GAME ROUTINE:
## THE KEY TO LETTING GO OF GOOD AND BAD

When the game is over, I go through a specific post-game routine in which I evaluate the good and the bad of my performance. This is a significant perspective change that I have made in the last year. I used to evaluate my performances as good or bad and have since learned that evaluating as good _and_ bad is less emotional and more matter of fact. Removing the emotion from post performance evaluation leads to more honest feedback for performance improvement.

In hockey, you often play on consecutive nights and you have got to be able to bounce back after a loss and play with confidence the next night.

When I get off the ice, whether after a game or practice, I always try to get some food or a protein shake in me as soon as possible to help with recovery. I keep a gallon of chocolate milk at the rink so that when I get off the ice I can fill a glass to start the recovery process.

I then get undressed and go right to the cold tub to try to help my body relax. I do three minutes in the cold tub and then three minutes in the hot tub. I then repeat with three in the cold and three in hot. It is something I learned from reading a great article on Roy Halladay, the major league baseball pitcher, of whom I am a huge fan because of his commitment to the mental game and how hard he works physically.

After that last soak in the hot tub, I go and do about a 10 minute foam roll followed by a 20 minute static stretch, just to try and help me relax.

I then go to my stall in the locker room, where by that time, I am usually the last person to leave, so it is nice and quiet, and I take out my peak performance journal and make some notes about the game and my performance. Things I learned, things I did good and bad so that I can continue to learn about myself and the game.

## MENTAL IMAGERY:
## AN IMPORTANT PART OF PROCESS

After writing, I will lie on the floor and put my legs up on my stall and put a towel over my face. I will do this both post-practice and post-game and do mental imagery of specific aspects of my performance and will replay in my mind what I did well and if there was something I felt like I needed to do better. I always finish my mental imagery session by seeing positive outcomes. It is incredible how great you feel after doing the mental imagery, even if you do not feel like you had the greatest practice, or greatest game.

The brain processes information whether you vividly imagine it or physically experience it with the same psycho-neuro-muscular pathways so that your body and brain act like you have done what it is you see with your mind's eye. This is a critical part of my post-game routine that helps get my mind back in a positive mindset, and it definitely prepares me for the next day.

That short mental imagery session, that takes less than five minutes, does wonders for you as far as preparing you for what you want to do on the ice, but also gives you an opportunity to start snapping back into your "real world self" after the "hockey world self's" day is done.

I have learned that you want to have two selves, your real world self and your competitive self. Some call it being able to go from being the Boy Scout off of the ice to the bounty hunter on the ice.

The post-game routine helps me to get back to my personal life and all of the stuff that comes with being off-ice and just being myself. I see hockey as an escape from the real world and what is going on for the rest of the day. It allows you to play with a lot more consistency because you are just not holding onto everything in your life when you are on the ice. Having a routine frees you up to play in the moment.

## HOCKEY IS WHAT YOU DO, NOT WHO YOU ARE

A lot of players, early in their career, see themselves as hockey players only and this puts a lot of pressure on them to perform well because their self-image is wrapped up in how they perform on the ice. The "hockey is who I am" mentality puts a lot of pressure on yourself, and I recommend shifting to a "hockey is what I do" mentality so that you can turn all of the pressure of having to play well into pleasure of wanting to play well.

Hockey is not a job. Hockey is my passion. Hockey is my career, and the hardest part is when you walk out of the rink at the end of the day to leave it behind you. If you get married and have children, your family does not care as much about how you played as they need you to be Super-Dad when you walk into the house. You have got to be able to let go of the game, both good and bad and have the same amount of energy off the ice as you do on the ice. It is a different energy, but it is important to have energy in both areas of your life so that one does not suffer. Having a routine that you use, post-practice, to help you let go of the game, to leave it at the rink, is going to be huge in terms of your longevity and your ability to separate life on and off the ice.

I wish I had learned about separating life on and off the ice earlier in my career. In college, I got wrapped up in wanting to be too great, almost perfect, which is unattainable. At the start of my senior year, when I really made the conscious effort to separate life and hockey, I started to notice the dividends.

## HIP SURGERY PROVIDES TIME
## TO REFLECT AND LEARN

After my hip surgery, I got to spend a lot of time on the mental game, because I could not be doing physical things. If there is a piece of inexpensive experience I can pass on, it would be to take that time to do the mental conditioning work and develop your mental game as well as your physical game.

You can put all the time you want in the gym and on the ice, but without a strong mind and putting in the work on your mental game and developing the awareness you need to know where your mind is at in competition, you are not going to reach your maximum potential in hockey or any sport for that matter.

## TALENT IS OVERRATED

If talent was everything, every first-rounder would make it to the NHL or every first-rounder would make it in Major League Baseball. In baseball only 47% of the guys drafted in the first round make it to the big leagues. Less than that have an average Major League career of 3 years. It is probably less than 30%. Talent is not everything. It comes down to who are the guys who can stay healthy? Who are the guys that are going to stay motivated through the grind of the season? And who are the guys that are going to play consistently at their best?

Having routines helps you to be consistent, helps you to stay motivated, because you are able to separate hockey being what you do versus who you are, and having a routine increases your chances of staying healthy.

## SUCCESS IS NEVER AN EASY JOURNEY

Making a career as a professional athlete is never easy. The struggles you go through can either make you bitter and cause you to quit or they can inspire you to get better.

The struggles I have faced personally have been more of a challenge than what I have faced on the ice and have definitely made me more mentally tough as a person, not just as a hockey player. To go through adversity and test the limits of how much you really want something in life teaches you a lot about yourself and your sport. Walls and challenges are put up, not to keep you from achieving your goal, but to test your will and how badly you want something.

An outcome goal of mine since turning pro has been to get to the American Hockey League. That finally happened last year and I have the same outcome goal this year. I completely expect to get back there based on, not only where my talent levels are, but where my mind is at and just putting in the hard work and letting the outcome take care of itself.

I trust my preparation and my routines. I trust that my process for performance is as good as anyone's and that, in time, my career goals will take care of themselves if I take care of the process.

## LEARNING BY WATCHING VIDEO

I was watching a video on the NHL Network called NHL 36 where they followed NHL star Nicklas Lidstrom, arguably one of the best defensive players of all-time in the NHL, for 36 hours. They asked his coach Mike Babcock, "What makes Nick Lidstrom so good every day and allows him to have a 20+ year career and play until he is 41-42-years old?" Babcock said, "Well, most guys get bored with the grind. Somehow, Nick has found a way to enjoy and have fun doing the same, exact thing every day."

When Babcock said that, it was one of those "Aha" moments where you have got to find what works for you and what is going to excite your mind every morning to want to do that routine. Once you find that, it is pretty inspirational. If you can stay dedicated to the process, you will start seeing some good results.

## MENTAL GAME TRANSCENDS INTO LIFE

The mental game has helped me to deal with adversity in life and the grind and challenges outside of hockey. Whether it is dealing with relationship issues, dealing with family life stress, or dealing with injuries, the mental game skills that you learn on the ice help you as much, if not more, off the ice.

My dad was by far my best friend, and a huge mentor of mine. He did everything he could to help me chase after my own goals and dreams. He passed from ALS, Lou Gehrig's Disease, in the summer of 2012.

I had severely struggled with his death for a long time. Unfortunately, I did not recognize that I had the answers as to how to best deal with the loss of my father.

I did not do a good job of separating Mike Spillane, the hockey player (my competitive self, aka bounty hunter) and Mike Spillane of everyday life (my real self, aka Boy Scout). I was so focused on trying to make him proud through hockey versus just enjoying the game and being a good son at the same time, knowing that would be enough to make him proud, that I suffered both athletically and lifestyle-wise.

Once I was aware enough to see that I had the answers already in front of my face, and that I could use the mental game for my everyday life, things started to turn around. It is just simple things. You have to be able to separate the two, hockey and life.

I show up to the rink, turn my cell phone off immediately and start snapping-in to being the hockey player. When it is time to come out of being the hockey player, the cell phone comes on. I have really made a point of making sure I recognize the things that I have control over and the things I do not have control over.

**CAIN'S COACHING POINT:**
What do you do as a routine to help you separate from your real self to your competitive self and from your competitive self, back to your real self?

_____

_____

**THE BOY SCOUT:**
How do you want to be remembered as your "real self" aka "the Boy Scout"–the person who you are outside of the competitive arena?

_____

_____

**THE BOUNTY HUNTER:**
How do you want to be remembered as your "competitive self" aka "the bounty hunter"? The person who you are inside of the competitive arena?

_____

_____

## CONTROLLING WHAT YOU CAN CONTROL IS KEY

The statement "control what you can control" seems extremely simple, but if you do not have the awareness of the things that you can control, the things you cannot will eat you up very quickly and be very distracting.

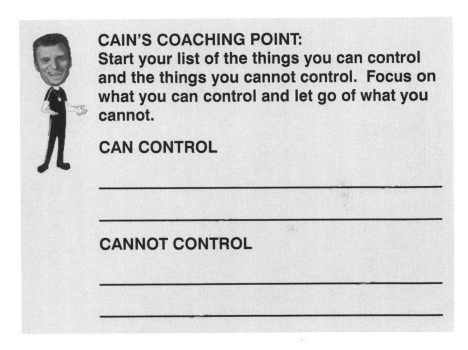

**CAIN'S COACHING POINT:**
**Start your list of the things you can control and the things you cannot control. Focus on what you can control and let go of what you cannot.**

**CAN CONTROL**

_____

_____

**CANNOT CONTROL**

_____

_____

I make it a point to write down in my peak performance journal the things that I know I can control and the things I know I cannot control. When I feel like I do not have control over a situation, I find somebody that I am close with – a teammate, a friend, and talk it out as if we are talking about an issue someone else is having. When you talk about an issue as it if is someone else's, it gives you that ability to not talk and think with emotion, but with logic.

## EMOTION CLOUDS REALITY

The second you get wrapped-up into that emotional thought, you usually end up making a poor decision or things snowball on you. Just like sports, life is the same way. Unfortunately, life is a lot more real, and the consequences in life are usually a lot worse. If you let those things that you cannot control wrap you up, it snowballs every time, and most definitely gets worse.

## RESPONSE-ABILITY

I think that you have a responsibility as an athlete to give yourself the best chance for success by making sure that you know very clearly what you have control over and what you do not. If there is a negative thing that happens, you have the ability to choose your response to that situation. You can stop, take a breath, pause and choose your best response. Response-ability is really respond-ability, your ability to choose how you respond in any situation. The best thing you can do when faced with a negative situation is to take a minute, breathe and get back into a strong mindset to make sure you make an educated decision versus an emotional one.

When you talk about losing a family member or a friend to cancer or terminal illness, you can fight, but it is a fate that you do not necessarily control the outcome of – just like hockey. You have got to just stick with the present moment, one day at a time, focus on the process over the outcome, control what you can control and stay positive.

Take that deep breath and make sure you are turning all of those "have to's" into "want to's". Not having to go to the rink, not having to do things, but wanting to do it. Just that psychological shift will turn it around for you and make it more positive.

## THE MAN IN THE GLASS

Regardless of whether or not I make it to the NHL, when I take those skates off, I want to be able to look in the mirror and have no regrets because I can honestly say there is nothing else that I could do to help me get to where I want to go. I think the true measure of success is that when your career is over, if you can look at the man in the glass and can say, "There is nothing else I could have done," you have truly been successful.

It's that perspective of no regrets that definitely makes it easier to play with a clear mind. I have noticed the difference drastically, especially coming into this year. My outcome goal is to be in the American Hockey League before the year is done, but right now I am focused on the process and what I need to do. The mental game has made a big difference in my career and it is like anything else. You have to work at the mental game, your routines, breathing, positive self-talk and thinking everyday to start seeing the benefits of your mental conditioning in competition.

You can email Mike Spillane at michael.spillane33@gmail.com and follow him on twitter at @spills33.

# CHAPTER #10 REVIEW

☐ Inexpensive experience and giving back to the game

☐ Remaining calm is essential

☐ Routines are key for consistent performance

☐ Emotional balance, relaxed intensity and breathing

☐ Focal point: key part of routine

☐ Physical ability is important but not enough

☐ Routines, pre-game, pre-shift, pre-period

☐ In game releases

☐ Confidence is a choice

☐ Post game routine: the key to letting go of good and bad

☐ Mental imagery: an important part of process

☐ Hockey is what you do, not who you are

☐ Hip surgery provides time to reflect and learn

☐ Talent is overrated

☐ Success is never an easy journey

☐ Learning by watching video

☐ Mental game transcends into life

☐ Controlling what you can control is key

☐ Emotion clouds reality

☐ Response-ability

☐ The man in the glass

# WHO IS BRIAN CAIN?
## ABOUT THE MASTER OF THE MENTAL GAME

B rian M. Cain, MS, CMAA, is the #1 best-selling author of *Toilets, Bricks Fish Hooks and PRIDE: The Peak Performance Toolbox EXPOSED* and *So What, Next Pitch: How To Play Your Best When It Means The Most* and *The Mental Conditioning Manual: Your Blueprint For Excellence.*

An expert in the area of Mental Conditioning, Peak Performance Coaching, and Applied Sport Psychology, Cain has worked with coaches, athletes, and teams in the Olympics, the National Football League (NFL), National Basketball Association (NBA), National Hockey League (NHL), Ultimate Fighting Championship (UFC), and Major League Baseball (MLB) on using mental conditioning to perform at their best when it means the most.

Cain has also worked with programs in some of the top college athletic departments around the country, including Vanderbilt

University, the University of Alabama, Auburn University, the University of Tennessee, the University of Mississippi, Mississippi State University, Florida State University, the University of Iowa, the University of Michigan, the University of Maryland, , Oregon State University, the University of Southern California, Washington State University, Texas Christian University, Texas A & M University, Baylor University, The University of Houston, Coastal Carolina University, Yale University, and many others.

Cain has worked as a mental-conditioning consultant with numerous high school state, NCAA national and professional world championship winning teams and programs. He has delivered his award-winning seminars and presentations at coaches' clinics, leadership summits, and conventions all over the globe. As a former director of athletics, he is one of the youngest ever to receive the designation of Certified Master Athletic Administrator from the National Interscholastic Athletic Administrators Association.

A highly sought-after coach, clinician, and speaker, Cain delivers his message with passion, enthusiasm, and in an engaging style that keeps his audiences energized while being educated. Someone who lives what he teaches, Cain will inspire you and give you the tools necessary to get the most out of your career.

Find out when Cain will be coming to your area by visiting his calendar at www.briancain.com.

# HOW YOU CAN BECOME
# A MASTER OF THE MENTAL GAME
Cain offers a range of training materials to get you or
your team to the top of your game.
Available at www.BrianCain.com

## MASTERS OF THE MENTAL GAME SERIES BOOKS

### Champions Tell All:
### Inexpensive Experience From The Worlds Best
Cain provides you with all access to some of the World's
greatest performers. Learn from mixed martial arts world
champions and college All-Americans about mental toughness.

### The Daily Dominator:
### Perform Your Best Today. Every Day!
You get 366 Daily Mental Conditioning lessons to help you start
your day down the path to excellence. Investing time each day
with Cain is your best way to become your best self.

### The Mental Conditioning Manual:
### Your Blueprint For Excellence
This is the exact system Cain uses to build champions and
masters of the mental game and has helped produce NCAA and
High School, champions, MMA world champions, and more.

### So What, Next Pitch:
### How To Play Your Best When It Means The Most
A compilation of interviews with top coaches and players
where Cain teaches you their systems and tricks. Learn
from the insights of these masters of the mental game.

### Toilets Bricks Fish Hooks and PRIDE:
### The Peak Performance Toolbox EXPOSED
Go inside the most successful programs in the country that use
Cain's Peak Performance System. Use this book to unlock your
potential and learn to play your best when it means the most.

# PEAK PERFORMANCE TRAINING TOOLS

## The Peak Performance System: (P.R.I.D.E.) Personal Responsibility In Daily Excellence

This big, video-based training program is Cain's signature training program for coaches, athletes and teams. It will take you step by step to the top of the performance mountain.

## Diamond Domination Training : The New 4RIP3 System for Baseball and Softball

This training program is being used by 11 teams in the NCAA top 25 in college baseball and 8 of the top 25 in college softball. It will help you and your team to unlock your potential and play the best baseball and softball of your life.

## 4RIP3 MMA Mental Conditioning System

Get the techniques used by the best fighters in the world to and start bringing the fighter you are in the gym into the cage. It will help you unlock your potential, teach you drills to sharpen your focus and give you the confidence of a champion

## The Peak Performance Boot Camp

This introductory program will give you the tools, power, and mental toughness you need to be prepared for every game, every play, and every minute. Learn techniques to get the absolute best chance of maximizing your potential and getting the most out of your ability.

### And more at www.BrianCain.com/products

*"Cain has tapped into the mental side of performance like no one ever has."*

**Tom Murphy**
***President, The Fitness Zone Gym***

*"This is your blueprint for making excellence a lifestyle not an event."*

**Jim Schlossnagle**
***2010 National College Baseball Coach of The Year***

*"Cain's books, DVDs and audio programs will give you a formula for success between the ears."*

**Bob Tewksbury**
**Sport Psychology Consultant, Boston Red Sox**

*"If you make one investment in coaching excellence and impacting the lives of the youth you lead, this is the program you want to follow."*

**Clay Chournous**
**High School Football and Baseball Coach, Bear River H.S.**

*"This will not only help you on the field, it will help you in life."*

**Nate Yeskie**
**Assistant Baseball Coach, Oregon State University**

*"Brian Cain will give you and your team a system for playing at your best when it means the most."*

**Todd Whitting**
**Head Baseball Coach, Univ. of Houston**

*"This was the best presentation I have seen in all of my clinics/ conventions I have attended over the years. OUTSTANDING!!!"*

**Michelle Daddona**
**Riverside Community College**

*"The information you get from Brian is the highest quality and can benefit a team, an athletic department and coaches of all experience levels."*

**Bill Gray**
**Missouri Southern State University**

## CONNECT WITH CAIN

Your link to doing a little a lot, not a lot a little

*twitter.com/briancainpeak*

*facebook.com/briancainpeak*

*linkedin.com/in/briancainpeak*

*youtube.com/wwwbriancaincom*

*briancain.com/podcast*

## SIGN UP FOR THE
## PEAK PERFORMANCE NEWSLETTER

Cain's newsletter is full of information to help you unlock your potential and perform at your best when it means the most. Subscribe for free and get a bonus audio training.
*__www.BrianCain.com/newsletter__*

## VISIT CAIN ON THE WEB

THE OFFICIAL WEBSITE OF
**BRIAN CAIN**
PEAK PERFORMANCE EXPERT
MENTAL CONDITIONING COACH
#1 BESTSELLING AUTHOR
EDUCATIONAL LEADER

**www.BrianCain.com**

**Remember to go to
www.BrianCain.com/experience
for all the BONUS Mental Conditioning
material mentioned in this book.**

# NOTES:

# NOTES:

# NOTES:

# NOTES:

# NOTES:

# NOTES:

Made in the USA
Charleston, SC
02 August 2014